OR

Richard Peirce

DEDICATION

This book is dedicated to all the campaigners,
scientists, activists, advocates and others
who are engaged in marine conservation.
Healthy seas and oceans are vital components in
maintaining life as we know it on our planet. Thank
you for what you do, and please keep on doing it.

Best wishes, *Richard Peirce*

Published by Struik Nature
(an imprint of Penguin Random
House South Africa (Pty) Ltd)
Reg. No. 1953/000441/07
The Estuaries, No. 4, Oxbow Crescent,
Century City, 7441 South Africa
PO Box 1144, Cape Town,
8000 South Africa

Visit www.penguinrandomhouse.co.za and
join the Struik Nature Club for updates,
news, events and special offers.

First published in 2019
1 3 5 7 9 10 8 6 4 2

Publisher: Pippa Parker
Managing editor: Roelien Theron

Editor: Helen de Villiers
Designer: Janice Evans
Cartographer: Liezel Bohdanowicz
(pages 12–13)
Proofreader: Thea Grobbelaar

Reproduction by Studio Repro
and Hirt & Carter Cape (Pty) Ltd
Printed and bound by CTP Printers,
South Africa

Print: 9781775846420
ePub: 9781775846437

PHOTO CREDITS

Front cover: Breaching Orca off Gansbaai. (Wilfred Chivell)
Title page: At sea with the Simon's Town Boat Company. (Dave Hurwitz)
Page 3 (opposite): A stealth predator eerily reflected. (Dave Caravias)
Pages 4–5: Port and Starboard on patrol. (Dave Hurwitz)
Pages 14–15: The telltale collapsed dorsal fin that identifies
Port and Starboard. (Wilfred Chivell)
Pages 26–27: Some visitors get lucky and take
home amazing photographs. (Dave Caravias)
Pages 42–43: For the shark enthusiast, being this close
to a Great White is as good as it gets. (Dave Caravias)
Pages 88–89: A stark reminder of the vulnerability
of the 'king of the sea'. (Hennie Otto)
Pages 116–117: When the Great Whites left Seal Island in
False Bay, Sevengill (Cow) sharks moved in and, in turn,
were hunted by Port and Starboard. (Dave Hurwitz)
Back cover: Two Orcas, locally known as Port and Starboard, are
spotted here passing the lighthouse at Danger Point. (Wilfred Chivell)

Contents

Author's note

The real-life characters in this book have all been chosen because they represent different aspects of life in the cage-diving industry and in Gansbaai.

I have often referred to Gansbaai as 'Shark Town' and I recognise that in the town, and in the cage-diving industry, there is a huge diversity of interesting and engaging characters. I would like to have included many more, but of course this was not possible. My apologies to anyone I have left out who feels they should have been included.

There is no actual proof that Orca predation was responsible when the Great Whites first disappeared in early 2016. However, it is reasonable to assume that this was the case, and there is strong anecdotal evidence to support the contention, so I have started the story with these dramatic events. What followed is based on fact. The characters mentioned in this book all read it prior to publication, and all agreed it is an accurate account of the facts, and that the suppositions made in the absence of hard facts are logical.

Great White sharks attract thousands of visitors to Gansbaai every year.

Foreword

by Wilfred Chivell

Joining the cage-diving industry was originally more about operating a sustainable business than protecting sharks. This changed when I realised I was one of the few who was willing to carry out and sponsor scientific research on Great White sharks. Meeting Richard Peirce was very important to me; not only is he a conservationist – at the time we met he was chairman of the UK Shark Trust – but also someone who wrote stories that could change things. Writing about important issues must make a difference, and in our case the issue is wildlife. Wild fauna and flora are devastated by the continuous growth of the human population. Animals cannot speak for themselves; their evolution over millions of years has fine-tuned them to perfection and has enabled them to survive thus far – but evolution cannot keep pace with human destruction.

Threats to nature are not unique to our area – they affect all corners of our planet. There are some heartening stories of successful conservation projects, and some species only remain today due to the efforts of a few passionate committed people. I hope that books like this, and others by Richard, will help make a difference to our wildlife which is in such desperate need of help.

Gansbaai's story shows how a few live sharks can economically make or break a little town. An area known globally for the diversity of its marine life is now also known for its vulnerability. The recent past has taught us all a lesson that I hope we will not forget. Although only a few of us could be mentioned in the book, many more have played major roles over the years in developing Gansbaai's Great White shark cage-diving industry. We have become the guardians of Great White sharks in South Africa, and we need to ensure their survival as a critical apex predator. Their loss would affect the entire ecosystem, and the impact of recent events is already being seen.

Foreword

by Chris Fallows

Natural resources are under ever-increasing pressure from over-exploitation, poaching and lawlessness. The domino effect of removing or exploiting one life form, and the consequences it has on another, is graphically illustrated in *Orca*. The effects are far more wide ranging than could ever be expected. This book highlights the impact of human-induced changes at the highest level on the trophic scale.

Port and Starboard, the notorious Orcas that have wreaked havoc amongst Great White shark populations along the Cape coastline, didn't end up with their deformed dorsal fins by chance: Orcas are being illegally shot, particularly by the tuna and swordfish longlining boats. Man's over-exploitation of fisheries must be affecting their food sources, and human pollution dumped in the oceans has degraded their habitat.

We now have compromised animals coupled with dwindling natural resources, and to survive they have had to change their habits. In the case of these two Orcas, one change has been to alter their normal diet and hunt sharks in the shallows. If there is one super-predator on the planet that is adaptive, it is the Orca.

Orcas are not the only pressure on Great Whites. Demersal longliners are being allowed to wipe out smaller shark species and other normal food sources. For Great Whites these are catastrophic blows that may doom the species. A world-famous tourism industry is crumbling, and jobs are being lost – the opposite of what the South African government claims to achieve.

Richard's book follows the meltdown of both the ecosystem and the tourism industry; the characters are real and so is the story. *Orca* is a timeous and tragic reflection of the hand-in-glove relationship between over-exploitation and a government that is apathetic to the demise of its globally famous natural resources.

Acknowledgements

Kelly Baker	Lloyd Edwards	David Hurwitz	Christina Rutzen
Dave Caravias	Chris & Monique	Dr Alison Kock	Lalo Saidy
Wilfred Chivell	Fallows	Brian McFarlane	Alison Towner
Brenda du Toit	J.L. Fourie	Hennie Otto	Heidi van der Watt
Marine Dynamics	Denise Headon	Jacqueline Peirce	Bo & Mimi Wixted

Special thanks must go to Wilfred, Alison and Brenda at Marine Dynamics, who were hugely generous with their time and put up with endless phone calls, interviews and requests for help.

And, finally, thanks to everybody at Struik Nature who once again dealt with a difficult author with patience, and did a brilliant job putting this book together – Pippa Parker, Helen de Villiers, Janice Evans and Belinda van der Merwe. I apologise to anyone I have inadvertently left out.

Hennie Otto

Divers aboard *Slashfin*, waiting to get into the cage.

Preface

Things have changed a lot in the 20 years I have been visiting Gansbaai and Kleinbaai. From quiet beginnings, there are now eight full-time cage-diving operators taking thousands of people each year to the Dyer Island area to view Great White sharks. Their ecotourist customers arrive with varying ambitions and motivations; there are committed admirers for whom Great Whites are iconic and who can't get enough of them; nervous first-timers who set off anxiously – but often return as devoted shark fans; and thrill-seeking adrenaline junkies who want to get the T-shirt and boast about it.

Some believe that cage diving is exploitative, while others argue that ecotourism benefits sharks by giving them an ongoing, multi-use live value. Great Whites are listed as a protected species by the South African government and in many other countries too, including Australia and the United States of America. The species is also listed on Appendix II of the Convention on International Trade in Endangered Species of Wild Fauna & Flora (CITES). This listing forbids all but specific, controlled international

Shark Town from the air.

Generating income for hundreds of people offers the best possible protection for sharks.

trade monitored by CITES. Despite their CITES listings, some iconic land species like rhinos and elephants have continued being killed by poachers at alarming rates. In contrast, Great Whites in the Gansbaai area are watched over by a whole human community of guardian angels and 'gamekeepers' with a vested interest in their wellbeing. Generating tourism income for hundreds of people is the best protection they could have.

One cage-diving operator commented on the exploitation charge: 'Maybe we exploit the sharks but not in any negative way. They are there, and we take people to see them, and help get sightings by using chum, but they are free and come and go as they like. I think of it as non-invasive and it has no bad impact; everyone is a winner. The clients see the sharks, and we make a living, so we would protect them with or without a law.'

The 'if it pays it stays' issue is one of the great wildlife debates, on both moral and practical grounds. Mountain Gorillas in the Virunga Mountains in central Africa don't have to rely for their future on altruism or conservationists with consciences: each gorilla in Rwanda generates over a million dollars a year for the national economy. It may not be laudable that humans fight hardest for wild species when there is financial gain, but it is a fact that works well for both Rwanda's gorillas and Gansbaai's sharks.

I have watched once-sleepy Gansbaai become wide awake as shark cage diving has grown. And, as time passes and this community's reliance on sharks increases, so does the scale of the potential disaster if the sharks were ever to disappear.

RICHARD PEIRCE

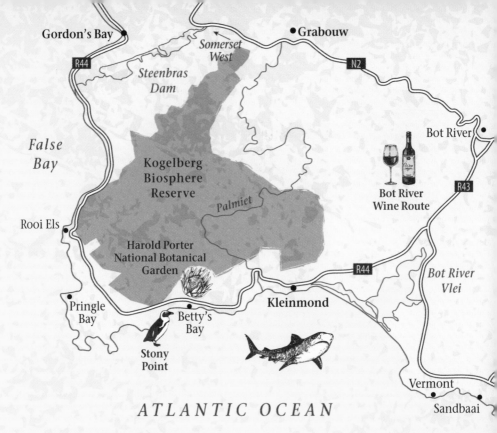

Gordon's Bay

Grabouw

Somerset West

R44

Steenbras Dam

N2

False Bay

Kogelberg Biosphere Reserve

Bot River

Palmiet

Bot River Wine Route

R43

Rooi Els

Harold Porter National Botanical Garden

R44

Bot River Vlei

Pringle Bay

Betty's Bay

Kleinmond

Stony Point

Vermont

ATLANTIC OCEAN

Sandbaai

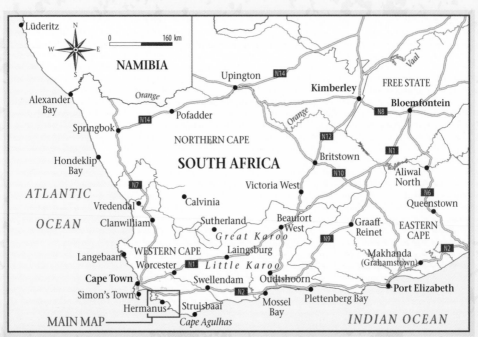

Lüderitz

N

W   E

S

0   160 km

NAMIBIA

Upington

N14

Kimberley

FREE STATE

Orange

Alexander Bay

N14

Pofadder

Orange

N8

Bloemfontein

Springbok

NORTHERN CAPE

N12

Britstown

N1

Hondeklip Bay

SOUTH AFRICA

N10

Aliwal North

N6

ATLANTIC

N7

Victoria West

Queenstown

OCEAN

Vredendal

Calvinia

Beaufort West

Graaff-Reinet

EASTERN CAPE

Clanwilliam

Sutherland

Great Karoo

N9

N2

Langebaan

WESTERN CAPE

Laingsburg

Makhanda (Grahamstown)

Little Karoo

Cape Town

Worcester

N1

Oudtshoorn

Port Elizabeth

Simon's Town

Swellendam

N2

Mossel Bay

Plettenberg Bay

Hermanus

Struisbaai

MAIN MAP

Cape Agulhas

INDIAN OCEAN

Vaal

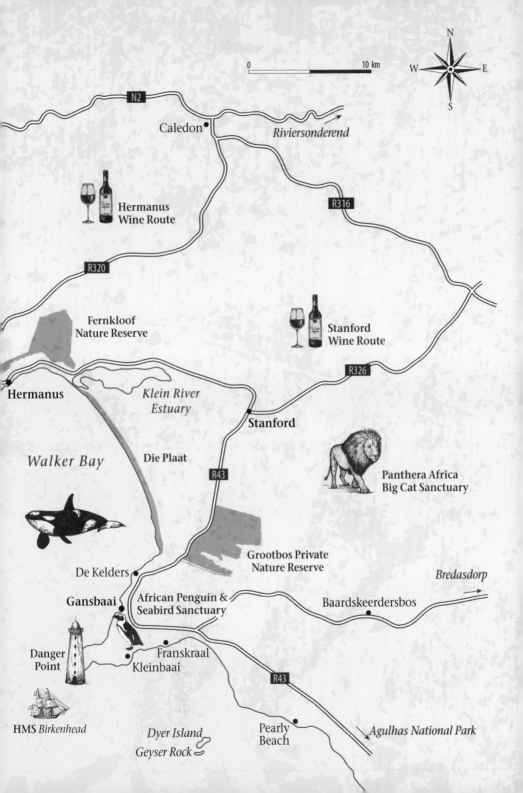

0   10 km

N
W   E
S

N2

Caledon

Riviersonderend

R316

Hermanus
Wine Route

R320

Stanford
Wine Route

Fernkloof
Nature Reserve

R326

Hermanus

*Klein River
Estuary*

Stanford

Walker Bay

Die Plaat

R43

Panthera Africa
Big Cat Sanctuary

De Kelders

Grootbos Private
Nature Reserve

Bredasdorp

Gansbaai

African Penguin &
Seabird Sanctuary

Baardskeerdersbos

Danger
Point

Franskraal
Kleinbaai

R43

Agulhas National Park

HMS *Birkenhead*

Dyer Island
Geyser Rock

Pearly
Beach

PART 1

CHAPTER 1

Shark Town

Sharks were part of the scene long before people settled along the coast of southern Africa, long before the village of Gansbaai was established, and long before the local population came to depend on these apex predators for their livelihood. To local residents, sharks seemed to have been a part of life forever ... but would this guarantee their survival into the future?

Dave Caravias

A Great White shark getting a close look at the cage and boat.

hark fishing has been practised in South Africa since the arrival of the early European settlers in the mid-17th century. Shark gill-net fishing first started off the KwaZulu-Natal coastline in the 1930s. Early landings of about 100 tonnes had risen steeply to 1,000 tonnes by 1940, thanks to the demand for shark-liver oil, which was a rich source of vitamin A.

Sharks have also been important contributors for many years to the economy of Gansbaai in South Africa's Western Cape. In 1939 a small factory was built here to process vitamin A from shark livers, and to extract the liver oil, which was used as a lubricant. The factory thrived during World War II but declined after the war ended.

Then, in 1950, Johannes Barnard, the principal of the local Gansbaai school, persuaded fishermen to get together and set up South Africa's first Fishery Co-operative. Finance was obtained from the Fisheries Development Corporation, the harbour was deepened, and a modern fish-meal factory was established here in 1952. The industry became a major employer, although Gansbaai was still a relatively quiet – even sleepy – Western Cape fishing town. And so it remained until the 1990s, when the influence of the Great White shark began to be felt as cage diving burgeoned and rapidly took over as the major local employer.

Shark Alley runs between Dyer Island and Geyser Rock, two small islands that are located 8 kilometres offshore from Gansbaai's neighbouring Kleinbaai harbour. Shark Alley is patrolled by Great White sharks, which prey on the 60,000 Cape fur seals resident in a colony on Geyser Rock. During the 1990s the Dyer Island area came to be acknowledged by scientists and film-makers as a great place to study and film the sharks, and documentary films introduced Great Whites to global audiences.

By the start of the new century, cage diving with Great Whites was attracting ever-increasing numbers of wide-eyed shark fans, and the 'shark town' of Gansbaai had started styling itself the 'Great White shark capital of

David Edwards

Shark Alley runs between Dyer Island and Geyser Rock.

Hennie Otto

Getting to see a shark breaching is a bonus for shark fans.

the world'. Nowadays, there are few people among Gansbaai's population of about 30,000 who don't have a connection to the ecotourism industry that has grown up around the iconic sharks.

In 1975 film director Steven Spielberg turned author Peter Benchley's story about a Great White shark into a suspense-packed worldwide blockbuster. The film *Jaws* chilled and thrilled audiences everywhere and cemented the Great White's position as the world's wildlife archvillain. In the fictional *Jaws*, the presence of a Great White threatened the prosperity of a New England summer resort town called Amity.

It is impossible not to be impressed by a Great White only a couple of metres away.

Dave Caravias

WHITE SHARK VENTURES
RESEARCH - EDUCATION - PRESERVATION

White Shark
Safaris

SHARK LADY SAYS

CARCHARIAS

Est.

SHARKLADY SAYS... PROTECT SHARKS!

SHARKLADY SAYS...STOP THE SLAUGHTER!!!

CAGEY GEAR
Clothing·Gifts·Curios

www.whitesharkprojects.com

☎ 076 245 5880

072 244 0(P)(S)

SHARK TEAM

WHITE SHARK
PUB & DISCO OPEN
DAILY
12h00 - 02h00.

LION LAGER	CASTLE/HANSA	BLACK LABEL
R10.20	R14.20	R16.20
EACH + DEP.	EACH + DEP.	EACH + DEP.
750mL RB.	750mL RB.	750mL RB.

SHARK DIVING
UNLIMITED
028 38

BARRACUDA

Dave Caravias

Great White shark ecotourism provides hundreds of jobs at sea and on land, and supports many others reliant on what has become Gansbaai's biggest employment sector.

A Great White shark investigating – not attacking – a shark diving cage.

A couple of decades later, in real life and across the globe, this same species of shark would prove to be a welcome and celebrated visitor, would launch tourism and bring prosperity to a small South African fishing village. Working out of the little harbour of Kleinbaai, cage-diving operators were ferrying tourists from all over the world out to Dyer Island for a date with the real 'Jaws': at peak times the eight established operators were each doing three trips a day, catering for up to 500 enthusiasts daily. And, conversely, it was the sudden *disappearance* of the Great Whites that would send an economic shiver through the 'Great White shark capital of the world'.

Hotels, booking agencies, guesthouses, restaurants, curio shops, taxis and others had all, to a degree, come to rely directly or indirectly on their unlikely toothy friends. Across Walker Bay from Gansbaai is the world-famous whale-watching town of Hermanus, where local businesses were also benefitting from the nearby cage-diving industry. The eight Gansbaai cage-diving operators directly employed about 200 people, and it is safe to say that over 1,000 people from the towns of Kleinbaai, neighbouring Gansbaai and Hermanus were, in one way or another, involved in Great White shark tourism and science.

For the first 16 years of the new century cage-diving operators flourished. They bought bigger boats; new support businesses opened, and a comfortable feeling of prosperity settled over the coastal towns. Year after year, profits were made and reliance on shark ecotourism increased. If, for any reason, Dyer Island's sharks ever disappeared, their absence would threaten Gansbaai as much as the presence of a fictional shark had threatened Amity Island.

Christmas is high holiday time in South Africa, and in late December 2015 Shark Town was buzzing. Gansbaai's high street was decorated with Christmas lights depicting sharks and other marine animals, the tills in local businesses were ringing, and seasonal gaiety combined with prosperity to produce an almost tangible air of happiness and wellbeing.

The vibe seemed to travel across the sea to the shallows near Dyer Island, where the cage-diving boats were busy chumming for sharks. There were five boats at anchor, and three others had left their cages at sea while they headed back to Kleinbaai to drop clients off and then collect their next groups of shark watchers. Four of the five boats had sharks around them, and crews were busy getting people in and out of cages, while others worked bait lines to keep the sharks interested.

It was a perfect summer day in every way: the sea was flat and calm, with only a slight swell, the sky was deep blue and cloudless and, unusually for

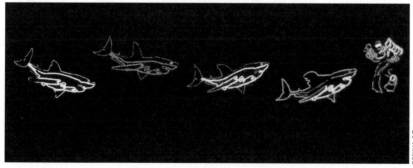

In the 'Great White shark capital of the world', sharks are even part of Christmas.

the area, the water was clear, affording good visibility. The sharks could be seen for several metres below the surface, and excited human cries and whoops split the air while dorsal fins sliced through the water.

The Great White House occupies a dominant position in Kleinbaai at the top of Geelbek Street, which is lined with cage-diving businesses all the way down to the water. It houses the cage-diving operator Marine Dynamics, the Dyer Island Conservation Trust (DICT) and Dyer Island Cruises. A woman wearing a blue jacket with 'Marine Dynamics' emblazoned on her back led a human crocodile, everyone wearing life jackets, out of the Great White House and down the slope towards the harbour, where a large catamaran named *Slashfin* waited to take them out to sea. The harbour and shore areas and Geelbek Street were all packed with people. Fluttering flags, colourful clothing and loud chatter combined to create a carnival atmosphere.

Richard Peirce

High season in Shark Town: boats come and go from Kleinbaai's little harbour.

The Great White House occupies a commanding position at the top of Geelbek Street.

Richard Peirce

At the lower end of the street, outside the White Shark Cage Diving premises, a tourist from the north of England was busy sending photos back home to her boyfriend. Then she called him, screaming with excitement as she described her encounter with Great White sharks.

It was just another day in Shark Town, and all was normal and right with the world. No-one could have guessed that an unforeseen danger was lurking out in the ocean and heading for Walker Bay, a danger that would shake Shark Town and threaten the futures of all those engaged in shark ecotourism. The possibility of the nightmare scenario that would soon develop had never entered people's minds. But the nightmare was approaching, and in early 2016 it would become reality – when the sharks disappeared.

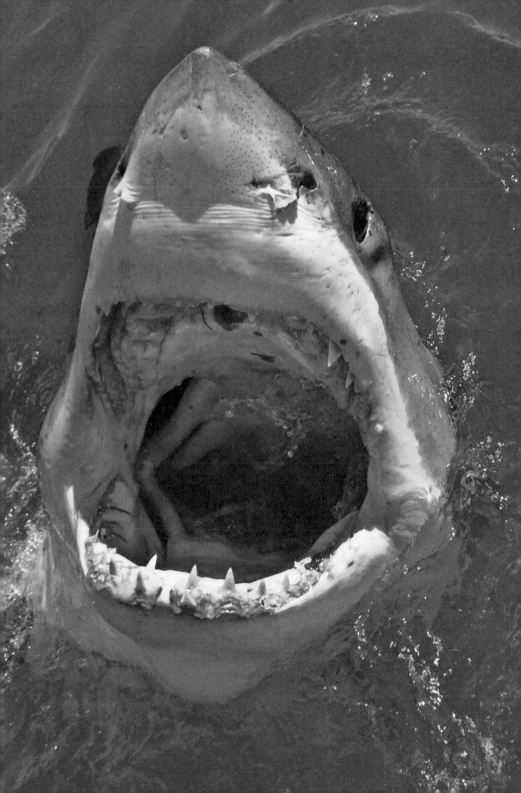

CHAPTER 2

Apex challengers

Unnoticed, unheralded and swimming below the radar were two denizens of the deep – a pair of Killer whales on the hunt. They would soon cause a monumental stir, not only in the deep, but also along the coastline of southern Africa as they went head-to-head with rival apex predators – Great White sharks. The dramatic repercussions would be felt both on and offshore.

Two Killer whales, later nicknamed 'Port' and 'Starboard', patrol near Gansbaai.

Orcas – beautiful, powerful and potentially deadly.

It was January 2016 and two iconic black-and-white super-predators were swimming south out of False Bay, from where they would travel southeast along South Africa's coast, across Walker Bay, heading for Danger Point. Over the next few weeks the two male Orcas would set in motion a chain of events that had the potential to dramatically alter the established patterns of life, both for sea creatures living in the Dyer Island area and for the local human population.

Often, the massive mammals swam side by side only a few metres apart, and at times they were not easily identifiable as Orcas. The huge, scythe-like vertical fin that identifies male Killer whales was not apparent on either animal – the fins of both had collapsed and were resting on their backs. One Orca's fin had fallen to the right, and the other's to the left. Human observers spotting the pair would be confused by the absence of the normal large, telltale fin.

The whales, of course, had no interest in how identifiable they were or in demonstrating their deadly supremacy. They were simply intent on feeding, and would soon be targeting not their traditional prey – seals – but their closest rival in the predator stakes. They turned into Walker Bay and cruised past Hermanus, where walkers on the coastal path, and those eating and drinking in cafés and restaurants were largely unaware of their passing.

A Scottish couple at Gearing's Point in Hermanus was busy watching and photographing dassies (Rock hyraxes) and seals resting on the rocks, while their young daughter stared out to sea. Suddenly the little girl's jaw dropped and she shouted 'Mummy, Mummy!', turning and grabbing her mother's skirt while still pointing out to sea. Her mother was slightly annoyed because at the moment her daughter had shouted, a dassie had been about to take food from her hand. Rather testily she hissed 'What,

Klaus Rainer Willner

Walker Bay, famous for Southern Right whales,
Great White sharks and now two particular Orcas.

darling?' and turned to look in the direction her daughter was pointing. But the Orcas had already gone, and a couple of minutes later their spouts would be scarcely visible some 300 metres further out to sea. No-one else in Hermanus would notice the huge marine mammals as they continued moving towards De Kelders on the other side of the bay. They were on their way to begin a battle of the giants.

Swimming parallel to the beach, they passed De Kelders, then Gansbaai, rounded Danger Point, and were patrolling near Dyer Island without anyone else having noticed them. Had their dorsal fins been standing erect, they would have been much more visible, but with their fins collapsed, they became stealth killers.

Collapsed dorsal fins are more commonly observed in captive, rather than wild, Orcas.

CHAPTER 3

The human players

The characters in this true-life story come from diverse backgrounds, some local, others from overseas. They have a range of personalities and a mix of training, skills and lifestyles. The one connecting thread that has pulled them all together in Shark Town is a passion for the sea and the Great White shark.

Hennie Otto

Scientist Alison Towner at work doing what, for her, is the best job in the world.

I n the Jordanian Red Sea port and resort city of Aqaba the sun was setting as the muezzin called the faithful to prayer. At the dining table in her small flat overlooking the sea, a young British scientist tapped away at her computer keyboard, typing an application for a job, while silently offering up prayers for good luck with her quest.

Alison Towner was a marine biologist with an obsession for sharks and, in particular, for Great White sharks. After finishing school in Manchester, she attended Bangor University in north Wales and did a degree in marine biology. With her degree in her pocket, she soon relocated to Aqaba to work as a dive instructor for a Jordanian company.

Now she was applying for what she considered to be her dream job – researching Great White sharks in South Africa. Dyer Island, offshore from Gansbaai, was the acknowledged global Great White hotspot, and Wilfred Chivell's Marine Dynamics and Dyer Island Conservation Trust organisations were looking for a research scientist.

Wilfred Chivell, Shark Town entrepreneur.

As she typed, she had a feeling deep down that she would get this job – although she hardly dared dream for fear of jinxing her chances in life's great job lottery.

The Red Sea was beautiful, and while working as a diving instructor, based in the port city of Aqaba, she had developed affection and respect for the Jordanian people. If she got the job she would be sad to leave, but the lure of the Great White shark outweighed the fun she was having in Jordan. She shut down her computer, then closed and covered it with a small towel to protect it from the dusty environment. She could have closed her doors and windows

Alison Towner – marine biologist, shark enthusiast.

and lived in the much cleaner air produced by her air conditioner – but when you are born in the north of England, you savour and appreciate sun and warm climates, and don't want to look at the world through glass if there are other options.

Sadly, Alison's father had passed away when she was only five years old, but there had been enough time for his influence on her to be telling. He was a writer for the *Manchester Evening News* and had harboured a lifelong passion for the sea and its creatures. He had written a book, an unpublished, Hemingway-style novel called *The Last Magical Fishing Trip*, that underlined his intense marine interest. One of his ambitions had been to see a Great White shark – an ambition that he hadn't lived long enough to achieve, but one that would inspire his daughter and set her on her eventual career path.

Two days after sending her job application to Wilfred Chivell, an email came back in response. Alison's fingers hovered over the keys while her mind fizzed with excitement – and prepared for disappointment. She clicked on the message and her eyes raced along the lines of the reply – her optimism had paid off, and she would soon be on her way to South Africa and the 'Great White shark capital of the world'.

She gave notice to her Jordanian employers and was soon heading south to fulfil her ultimate shark dream. Her mother had been nervous when Alison went to Jordan; now she was concerned again due to South Africa's reputation for being unsafe. But for Alison, nearly everything in her world was wonderful. Her only regret was that her shark-mad father wasn't there to share her happiness – he would have been so proud.

Alison's first 13 years in South Africa would be marked by great adventure, research and fun: she was realising her dream, and was

'THE GREAT WHITE SHARK CAPITAL OF THE WORLD' – quite a claim to live up to.

Boats packed with ecotourists had become the daily norm,
but soon a new reality would threaten to change everything.

making meaningful and valuable contributions to Great White shark science. But it would be two Killer whales that would make her a familiar face and name in marine circles around the world.

One might imagine someone who had been a diamond diver and a successful antiquities underwater treasure hunter to look like a cross between Johnny Depp as a pirate, Jacques Cousteau and Indiana Jones. Wilfred Chivell doesn't conform to this – or to any other stereotype. Wildlife – mainly marine – and its conservation is his abiding passion. Detractors would say he can be gruff and abrupt; fans would excuse this by saying he is single-minded and doesn't suffer fools gladly. If they could speak, the sea and its animals and birds would say 'thank you'.

Chivell's grandfather was born in Cornwall in the UK. Traditionally, the Cornish made their livings from agriculture and tin mining, and at sea from fishing and serving on ships. The Cornish are a fiercely independent and tough people, and to this day many consider Cornwall to be part of Britain rather than part of England – it is, after all, the only English county with its own flag and language. Wilfred Chivell may be a third-generation South African, but his family's Cornish background is still very much in evidence in his character and behaviour. He was born near Caledon in South Africa's Western Cape, where the family lived on a small dairy farm and were the main milk suppliers to the people of Gansbaai. Wilfred worked on the farm from his earliest years, and his father was a hard but fair taskmaster. He attended school in Gansbaai up to Grade Nine, and at 15 years old went to agricultural high school in Paarl as a boarding student. After school he did his four years' National Service in the police force, then went home to decide on what future path to follow.

A born adventurer, he soon spread his wings and spent the next few years diamond diving in Namibia, as well as wreck diving and spearfishing. Soon after the death of his father in 1981 he returned home to Gansbaai and started a small factory making bricks and blocks for building.

Then, on 1st January 1987, while out spearfishing with a friend, there came a real break: in shallow waters off Gansbaai, Wilfred found a cannon and other artefacts suggestive of a shipwreck. Instinct told the men this wreck was a significant find and, before returning to shore, they made careful note of its exact position. They went home with a roll of lead they had brought up from the seabed, and a piece of copper plate with the impression of a coin stamped on it. They sought advice from an experienced wreck diver in Gansbaai, who suggested they had found the *Nicobar* – a Danish ship that had foundered and sunk in 1783, and whose treasure had lain undiscovered all these years. A long process followed during which they registered the wreck, salvaged all they could and learnt everything possible about the value of their find.

In 1989 Wilfred, his friend and their archaeologist partner sold the coins from the wreck and each made several hundred thousand rand, which gave them the means to do what they wanted in life. Wilfred expanded his businesses, married and prospered. Then, in 1999 a difficult financial position in South Africa forced interest rates up to well over 20 per cent. The building industry was hit hard. Wilfred had always used all his money to expand, so he had no reserves. Companies that owed him money collapsed and went out of business, his cash flow dried up, and servicing his loans at such high interest rates became impossible. He was squeezed on all sides and foreclosure by the banks became inevitable. One moment, he ruled the world and was going forward like an express train, and the next, events beyond his control caused total financial collapse. In order to pay off the roughly 200 people who had been working for him, he sold everything he could, including his house. He had taken a very hard knock and it took a while to adjust mentally to the new realities, but adjust he did. Wilfred Chivell is not a man who stays down for long or has time for self-pity.

His wife had moved out and he was left with a bed, a TV, a chair, a fax machine, an old Land Rover and an inflatable boat. The boat was to be the key to the next stage in Chivell's life, when he started a company called Dyer Island Cruises and began taking tourists out whale watching, and to the Dyer Island seal colony. He began a process of putting himself back together again, and by 2005 he had bought a cage-diving company for viewing sharks underwater, called Marine Dynamics. The company was a significant cash generator, but Wilfred continued to run his valued whale-watching business in parallel. He loved and treasured the local

The African Penguin & Seabird Sanctuary near Gansbaai (top and above left), and Wilfred Chivell releasing a rehabilitated bird (above right).

environment and its wildlife, and recognised that both faced serious threats and challenges. This led him in 2006 to establish a conservation Non-profit Organisation (NPO) called The Dyer Island Conservation Trust (DICT). Then, in 2015, a decade after he had started with Marine Dynamics, he opened the African Penguin & Seabird Sanctuary, which is an affiliate of the DICT.

By now Wilfred Chivell was the biggest employer and, arguably, the most significant figure in the local marine sector. However, despite his success and the security that came with it, his financial crash of 1998 was ever present in his mind. He had learnt a very hard lesson and had learnt it well. Never again would he operate without cash reserves, and never again would he leave himself financially vulnerable. He knew that uncertainty and the unexpected were always waiting around the corner to ambush the unwary. What he didn't know was that two giant ocean predators were approaching and that they would threaten to destroy everything he had worked for.

Brian McFarlane's family has lived in and around Hermanus for six generations, ever since his great-grandfather, Walter McFarlane, arrived in South Africa from Scotland and started operating two fishing boats out of the old harbour in Hermanus. Brian's father was among the first to be involved in the abalone industry, and his first mini-factory was located in the family kitchen.

When Brian left school, it was not surprising that the sea called, and that he answered. He spent the first 20 years of his working life diving for diamonds, shipwrecks and abalone, or catching fish, and among the fish he caught were Great White sharks.

Cage diving with Great Whites was started in the late 1990s by Theo and Craig Ferreira, and the potential of this new form of ecotourism was quickly recognised by others. 'Shark Lady' Kim Maclean followed the Ferreiras and, before long, Brian McFarlane also started taking Great White

The McFarlane family has been part of the fabric of the area for six generations.

fans out to Dyer Island. His first cage-diving boat could take six people, and he crewed alone; he charged R300.00 a head, and did one trip a day. His operation grew steadily, and after 20 years he ran a much larger vessel with a crew of five, taking up to 40 shark watchers on each trip, and in high season doing three trips a day.

McFarlane called his company Great White Shark Tours, and its success and growth were an accurate reflection of the success and growth that cage diving had brought to Gansbaai, Kleinbaai and the wider area. In addition to the boat crew, his company employed another 18 people on shore doing marketing, administration, cooking, catering for guests, and performing various maintenance functions.

By 2014, the day-to-day operation of the boat was being handled by Brian's son who had grown up alongside the cage-diving industry. Down the years, generations of the family had had to strategise and struggle daily to make a living from the sea. Cage diving changed this: weather permitting, it provided a daily, year-round, money-making opportunity for the McFarlanes and for all those involved directly and indirectly in Great White ecotourism. It was a far cry from the harder, riskier lives led by the McFarlane forebears. As long as there were sharks, there would be tourists, and livelihoods would be safe. Or would they?

In 2000, 30-year-old Dave Caravias from England first visited Gansbaai to fulfil a long-held dream to see a Great White shark. Dave had only a few weeks earlier started a new job in Johannesburg – a three-month contract with a British-based IT consultancy. But now the hand of fate was hovering over the young English shark fan, and he could never have foreseen how unfolding events on this day would influence the course of his life.

He spent a wonderful morning out at Dyer Island with skipper and seasoned operator Jackie Schmidt, followed by lunch at a Gansbaai restaurant. Over lunch in Gansbaai, his gaze kept being drawn to a pretty young waitress who, quite unawares, held him spellbound. It so happened that a rugby match between South Africa and England was showing on TV. Dave saw a chance, called her over and proposed a wager with her: if England won she would go on a date with him. There was no agreement as to what would happen if South Africa won! – but there didn't need to be because England won the match, Dave won the bet and a date with Elna, who would later become his wife. That day, everything changed; he had fallen in love with a beautiful girl, with a new country, and with Great White sharks.

Dave's original assignment stretched to over a year before his company told him, in early 2002, that he was being sent back to the UK. However, by this time Dave had become entrenched in South Africa, which had become home and was where he saw his future. He handed in his notice and, together with Elna, started to look for ways to make a living in his adopted country. The shark cage-diving industry seemed a promising field, and so he and Elna decided to open a guesthouse offering accommodation to visiting cage divers.

A loan from Dave's UK bankers allowed them to buy a plot of land on Ingang Street in De Kelders, a village next door to Gansbaai, and they constructed an interesting circular building for use as a guesthouse, which they named the Roundhouse. He was a shark fan, his target customers were shark fans, and it felt appropriate that he should enter the shark-related market. He approached cage-diving operators to make sure they knew there was now a guesthouse offering services specifically tailored to the needs of their clients.

The Roundhouse, Dave Caravias' guesthouse in De Kelders.

The response was encouraging but bookings only really took off in September 2003 when Dave set up his own booking agency. **Sharkbookings.com** was initially conceived to facilitate bookings for the Roundhouse, but it quickly expanded and developed into an agency covering shark-diving destinations right up southern Africa's eastern coast, all the way to Mozambique.

The Caravias family flourished and expanded with the birth of their two daughters. Dave didn't regret his decision to move to South Africa. He had built a successful new life in a place he loved and now called home, and this new life involved him with the sharks he had dreamt of since he was a child.

Dave Caravias fatbiking with clients in dunes near De Kelders.

The sharks brought him visitors from all over the world and accounted for over 90 per cent of those who stayed at the guesthouse. As long as there were sharks, there would be visitors. It never occurred to him that the sharks might one day disappear.

Christina moved to Gansbaai in 1990, where she met and married commercial fisherman Frank Rutzen. Her new husband skippered his own boat, and Christina enjoyed going out fishing with him daily, until her pregnancy with their first child put an end to her trips.

In 1996 Frank started working with skipper Jackie Schmidt on his cage-diving boat and, like so many others in Gansbaai, the Rutzen family's future became tied to the fast-expanding cage-diving ecotourism industry. Although Christina was a full-time mother, she undertook various jobs supporting cage-diving operators, and then became manager in a local restaurant. In 2008, she applied for

Frank and Christina Rutzen, committed townspeople.

45

a job running the newly created harbour master's office in Kleinbaai, the little port where the cage-diving operators launch their boats – and she got it. Now harbour master, she was an integral part of the daily life of all Shark Town's operators. The whole Rutzen family were, in one way or another, involved with Great White sharks: Frank as a cage-diving skipper, Christina running Kleinbaai's harbour, and Frank's brother Mike working on cage-diving boats – until he got his own operator's licence and became world-famous as a free diver with Great Whites.

Storm clouds over Walker Bay.

For the Rutzens, when the new decade began in 2010, life and work were up and running. There were no apparent dark clouds on the horizon for the hard-working citizens of Shark Town. There was no way anyone could have forecast that, within a few years, storm clouds would gather that would shatter the future they had thought to be secure.

Stanley Carpenter

CHAPTER 4

An old man's hunch

Today's business is conducted in the fast lane. But those who have already spent a lifetime observing the world, gathering experience and drawing conclusions – those with the wisdom of age – often have much to teach us.

The little museum on the beach at Franskraal.

A small beachside museum in Franskraal, a village lying to the east of Gansbaai, is owned and curated by J.L. Fourie. During the 1990s and early in the new century, he watched as Shark Town's prosperity grew.

By 2016 Fourie was 81 years old, making him one of very few people who could remember the times when sighting Great White sharks around Dyer Island was perhaps not the near certainty that Shark Town's modern inhabitants had come to regard as normal.

He could remember when life in Gansbaai had been much harder – when local families had struggled to make their living doing artisanal fishing, working in the fish-processing factory, diving for abalone, shark fishing, collecting guano and cutting kelp. Today's young people were living in a very different world from that of their forebears who, even just 50 years ago, were often barely surviving hand to mouth.

He recalls a time in 1994 when, while working on Dyer Island collecting guano, he saw three Orcas patrolling on the land side of the island. The old man's job involved guano, not sharks; but seeing sharks was part of daily life, and his impression then was that there were fewer, or even no, sharks around while the three Orcas were present.

For the next 20 years or so, Orcas were not seen in the area, and Great Whites were present most of the time. Visitors could be assured of a more-than-90 per cent chance of seeing them.

Instances of Orcas preying on Great Whites have been documented in many places. But other than the old man sitting in his museum on the Franskraal beach, few would remember the possible connection between the presence of Orcas and an absence of sharks. Were the memories of an old man accurate? Had he correctly identified the Orcas back in 1994, and had the sharks actually left the area?

If Fourie's memories were accurate, the return of Orcas to the bay would cast a dark shadow over Shark Town and the prosperity of its people.

A cannon from the *Birkenhead* (see page 83).

CHAPTER 5

The Sevengill mystery

Finding shark carcasses on the seabed in a protected area sends out alarm signals. It is time for those who monitor our ocean and its inhabitants to step in and investigate.

Simon's Town Harbour in False Bay.

In 2014, in False Bay at a popular dive site called Castle Rock Reserve near the naval port of Simon's Town, divers started coming across the bodies of Broadnose Sevengill sharks (Cow sharks) lying on the seabed. They were in various stages of decomposition and appeared to have been attacked and killed. The question was, by what, and why?

Marine biologist Dr Alison Kock came to hear of the reports and examined photos and videos of the carcasses, but she was unable to learn much from the available evidence, particularly as most of the carcasses were already decomposing. One photo, however, showed such a neat, clean wound in the shark's belly that Alison thought it had possibly been done by a fisherman with a knife. The Castle Rock Reserve is a protected area (situated to the south of Simon's Town), so any possibility that sharks were being killed there by humans had to be investigated.

In April 2016 Alison and her team were called in to examine another carcass. These remains were fresh and they were able to discern tooth marks on both pectoral fins, and the liver was missing. Over the next few weeks several more Sevengill shark carcasses were found and examined, and Kock concluded they were being preyed on by Orcas. She was later quoted as saying: 'It looks as if at least two Orcas had to have worked together. We saw the bite marks on the pectoral fins and then the shark was torn open to the pectoral girdle. Based on that examination, it seems the Orcas are biting on the pectorals, ripping the shark apart and then taking its liver out.'

Some months earlier, Alison had been diving at Castle Rock when she had encountered two distinctive Killer whales. They were distinctive because both of them had collapsed dorsal fins: the fin of one of them flopped to the left, and that of the other to the right. It was this sighting and the necropsies (animal autopsies) she later performed that fed Kock's suspicion about Orcas being the mystery killers.

Dave Hurwitz, who named the two Killer whales.

Dead Sevengill (Cow) sharks provided the first clues.

Simon's Town-based naturalist and marine wildlife tour skipper Dave Hurwitz first saw Orcas in False Bay in 2009, when he spotted them in the town harbour, right beside his boat. Further sightings followed and, in 2015 near Seal Island in False Bay, Hurwitz saw the two Orcas with their collapsed fins. 'I named them "Port" and "Starboard". The fin of one of them flops over to the left, and the fin of the other to the right. I named them so that it would be easy to re-identify them', said Hurwitz. These names stuck and it wouldn't be long before even just the mention of 'Port and Starboard' would be like a kick in the stomach for people in the Western Cape making their livings from shark ecotourism.

While the experts and the practitioners of cage diving remained oblivious, young Alice Farraday, on holiday in South Africa from Edinburgh, had seen Orcas pass close in to Gearing's Point in Hermanus, which lies further east along the coast. In her excitement she had disturbed a dassie (rock hyrax) that her mother was hand feeding, and then had not stopped talking about her sighting all day. She sensed that her parents didn't really believe that she had seen two huge black-and-white 'fish' swimming past, close to where the family was standing. She didn't know that Orcas aren't fish, but she did know what she had seen, and her parents' apparent disbelief merely strengthened her determination to convince them. She returned to the subject repeatedly over the next couple of days, until the family happened to walk past a Hermanus book shop; Alice stopped in her tracks and pointed at the shop window, 'There, see, I told you!' The little girl was pointing at a picture of a pod of Orcas on the front cover of a nature book. She smiled smugly, as if to say, 'You didn't believe me, but I knew I was right'. Alice had just correctly identified the two Killer whales!

At this very moment the two animals were approaching Dyer Island from the west. Although adept at hunting co-operatively, and although they had a varied diet and often fed opportunistically, today they were on a specific mission: hunting Great Whites. Their goal was to extract the large shark liver, which can account for up to 24 per cent of the shark's body weight.

There were no squeaks or other noises between Port and Starboard as they patrolled their hunting ground – the element of surprise would be crucial. As the late afternoon sun seemed to accelerate towards the horizon, the pair sensed the presence of a Great White, using echolocation to pinpoint its precise location. The Great White seemed unaware of their approach, and the attack that followed was fast, brutal and deadly. The waters around Dyer Island became the scene of a mighty clash between two giant apex predators. It would not be the last such clash.

Sandra Hoerbst

Dyer Island's inhabitants provide a rich food source for Great Whites; now the sharks themselves are about to become a menu item too!

53

CHAPTER 6

The enigma

Families depend on regular income, and communities and services need ongoing revenue streams. What happens when a stable financial position turns overnight into a lottery?

Hennie Otto

Before the arrival of the Orcas in the Walker Bay area, Great Whites were the undisputed 'kings of the seas'.

All the boats put to sea on Tuesday, 5th January 2016 – and they all drew a blank.

Tuesday, 5th January 2016 started like any other day for Shark Town's cage-diving industry. All eight boats set off from Kleinbaai for the first of their habitual two or three daily trips.

The Great White sightings success rate was usually very high. Some days there were many sharks, and all the boats would be pumping with activity. Other times the sharks were scarce, and some boats would enjoy a sighting, but others not; and sometimes they would see sharks on one trip but not on the next. But there were sometimes blank days, so when none of the boats managed to attract a single shark that Tuesday, it didn't immediately ring any alarm bells.

On board Marine Dynamics' boat *Slashfin*, marine biologists Alison Towner and Kelly Baker were explaining to the disappointed would-be cage divers that the sharks were wild, and that sightings therefore couldn't be guaranteed. But they were welcome to take a voucher, which would give them a free trip another day.

An hour later *Slashfin* was heading back out to sea with a new group of enthusiasts, all aware of the failure of the last trip, and hoping to have better luck. While the crew chummed, Alison and Kelly talked to their visitors about Great Whites, their life history, habits and diet.

Alison's huge admiration, almost her love, for these animals was evidenced by the way she spoke and the sparkle in her eyes. When not answering questions or pointing out things of interest, she was silent as she gazed across the water. She didn't know why but she had a peculiar feeling that something was wrong, or something new was happening that she didn't understand: the sharks were missing. This had happened many times before, but this time the feeling was different; there was something sombre, indeed almost threatening in the air today. She looked across towards Dyer Island, and noted all the other familiar cage-diving boats riding at anchor close by. Everything seemed fine and normal, as it was every day, so why couldn't she shake this feeling of foreboding? She suppressed an involuntary shudder and turned and smiled at her clients; she had a job to do.

Slashfin made its way back to shore an hour later and for the second time that day they had to deal with the disappointment of the visitors. It was always wonderful to see people's reactions on their first encounters with Great White sharks: awe, excitement, wonder and happiness would play across the faces of cage divers and deck watchers alike. Alison really enjoyed seeing people become Great White shark fans, and so she keenly shared the disappointment when they were not seen.

Richard Peirce

Optimism was high each time the boat left Kleinbaai,
but disappointment hung heavily in the air on its return.

After the third and last trip of the day had also proved blank, *Slashfin's* crew decided to detour back to port via Dyer Island and spend a little time chumming the shallows along the adjacent beach, hoping to find the sharks had returned. Their efforts were rewarded when they had a brief sighting of a large 4-metre male Great White. At least the visitors on board had seen a shark, even if they hadn't been able to cage dive with it.

To have three virtually blank trips, one after the other, and involving all the boats, was by no means unknown, but it was unusual.

Dave Caravias' day had started badly. One of his staff at the Roundhouse hadn't turned up for work, which, because the guesthouse was full, meant more work for everyone else. He left the guesthouse at 8:30 a.m. and went to his office in Gansbaai where he ran **Sharkbookings.com**. Computer glitches had made for an annoying morning, and when he got back to the Roundhouse just after lunch he couldn't find his wallet. He thought he must have left it in the office and decided to go back and get it. When he opened his car door and saw it on the driver's seat, he decided to take this as an omen that the day was now going to get better. Dave is an unstoppable optimist: for him even the darkest clouds will have silver linings somewhere, and all negatives can be turned to positives. His enthusiasm for sharks, for life and for people is infectious, and this positivity would be needed today as his disappointed guests returned to tell their tales of woe.

His 18 guests had been out on three different boats and all had reported having seen no sharks. On most days they had photos and films of Great Whites to show him, and he would share their excitement as they enthused about their encounters. This was not a day on which to regale them with tales of his own shark adventures as it might simply depress them even more.

It wasn't too long ago that Dave had been a visiting shark fan himself, on that first, auspicious trip to Dyer Island with skipper Jackie Schmidt.

His interest in sharks had not diminished, so whenever he listened to his guests relating their adventures his enthusiasm was genuine. Today, his disappointment was as great as theirs. In spite of the company's offers of return vouchers, of his 18 guests, only two couples would be able to go back to sea the following day, hoping for better luck; the others all had preplanned schedules and couldn't delay their departures. He felt sorry for one guest in particular, a Swede who had taken time out of a business trip to Durban and had planned a detour south to fulfil a long-held ambition to see a Great White. This guest had now used his only spare day, and would have to return to Sweden having missed this dream of a lifetime.

Dave listened and sympathised with those who had lost out, and slowly his infectious enthusiasm dispelled the disappointment. And for those who could stay on – tomorrow was another day and it would be a great day. At least that is what Dave hoped as he silently prayed for plenty of shark sightings.

His hopes were in vain. January ticked by and none of the cage-diving boats reported shark sightings. Because there had been times before when sightings had been sporadic or had briefly stopped altogether, there was initially disappointment rather than real concern. For the first couple of days without sharks the eight operators carried on accepting bookings and putting to sea regularly. But as the days went by, three trips became two, and two trips became one. Then, as social media, blogs and TripAdvisor broadcast the news, the visitors all but dried up.

None of the operators wanted to take people out in the knowledge that the chances of seeing sharks, let alone cage diving with them, were almost non-existent, so they stopped doing trips with paying customers. However, the operators themselves continued going to Dyer Island and combing the shallows along the beach, and they chummed, hoping to find the sharks had returned. Marine Dynamics had set up a programme called 'International Marine Volunteers', and every other day the

The volunteers were full of hope and excitement at the start of each trip.

volunteers went to sea and chummed in the places where Great Whites were normally seen. There was excitement and anticipation at the start of each trip but, by the time they returned to Kleinbaai after another sharkless day, despondency had taken over.

Small communities in which many people make their livings in the same way are inevitably close knit. As harbour master, Christina Rutzen had a particularly inclusive view of Shark Town and cage diving: not only were her husband and brother-in-law directly employed in the industry, she also had daily contact with all the boats and their crews as they came and went from 'her' harbour.

From her little office at the top of the slipway at Kleinbaai harbour Christina watched the boats launching and going to sea, always full of hope on the outwards journey. By the time they returned, she already knew from their radio calls that no sharks had been seen. Christina's husband Frank was the skipper of *Great White*, a vessel operated by a company called Supreme Sharks, and not an evening went by without Frank and Christina discussing the situation before going to bed, hoping the next day would be different.

Christina was finely tuned in to the moods and feelings of those in her community. The sharks were sure to come back, weren't they? She hoped so – they had always come back before. But for some reason she couldn't explain, there was something different about the absence of sharks this time.

Port and Starboard had been hunting for Great Whites in the waters around Dyer Island since about the beginning of January. Every day their shark prey had become more wary and more difficult to kill, and now, after about a week, most of the sharks had fled from the threat of the superior predator.

Port and Starboard would soon become unwelcome
visitors to Dyer Island's surrounding waters.

Dolphins are also on the menu for Killer whales.

Meanwhile, no-one apart from the little Scottish girl on holiday in Hermanus was aware of the Orcas' presence in the Gansbaai area. Perhaps this was because their collapsed fins made them more difficult to see, or perhaps it was just chance. But because no-one had seen Port and Starboard along this particular stretch of the coast, no-one thought to connect the absence of the Great Whites with the dead Sevengill sharks Alison Kock had examined in False Bay, and which she strongly suspected of having been killed by Orcas. So the disappearance of the sharks in Gansbaai would remain an enigma for several months.

The Orcas wasted no time: they hunted and killed, and by 7th January they had gone, leaving behind them the puzzle of the disappearance of the Great Whites, and increasing numbers of people worried about their futures. The absence of the sharks was the most important thing in the lives of Shark Towners. In homes, coffee shops, restaurants and bars it was always part of the conversation as everyone put forward theories explaining the mystery of their disappearance.

Sunday 17th January was a fine blue-sky day with an easterly wind causing slightly choppy conditions. The Marine Dynamics volunteer group went to sea to do their alternate-days shark recce. The levels of enthusiasm and expectation had started to wane, but young volunteers having an adventure are rarely gloomy, so their chatter was incessant as *Slashfin* made her way out towards the island.

Chumming operations started and just in case a Great White turned up, the shark cage was lowered into the water. The first two hours slid by and the motivation of the observers was flagging when a volunteer jokingly suggested to one of the girls that she should jump in and swim around a bit, because that would be sure to either scare the sharks off for all time, or bring them back! The laughter had hardly died when cries of 'shark' caught the attention of all those on board, and a familiar shadow passed under the cage. The juvenile male shark did not stay, but a short while later a second shark also put in a brief appearance, and those on board the Dyer Island Cruises vessel *Dream Catcher* also saw a shark in the shallows.

Long before *Slashfin* was being pulled onto her trailer in Kleinbaai Harbour, a radio call from her skipper Hennie Otto had given harbour master Christina Rutzen the good news. Broad grins lit the faces of the volunteers as they disembarked. They could hardly wait to tell everyone they met that the sharks were back.

Following the volunteers as they walked up the slope to the Great White House, Alison and her fellow marine biologist Kelly Baker were deep in earnest conversation. They were elated at having seen the sharks, but their relief was tempered with caution.

News travels fast, and by that evening Shark Town's operators were all accepting bookings again, and some were planning trips for the very next day. However, the caution that had tempered Alison and Kelly's relief proved to be appropriate. Although 18th January was a perfect day, no sharks were seen by any of the boats that went to sea.

Cries of 'shark!' caught the attention of all those on board.

What those on shore did not know was that Great Whites had already been starting to move back into the waters around Dyer Island on Friday 15th January, but there were only a few of them at first, and they were tentative, which was why on the 16th none of the three boats that did chumming recces had seen them. The Marine Dynamics volunteers were right when, on the 17th, they thought the sharks were back. What they also didn't know was that in the late afternoon on the 17th, a pod of six Orcas cruised close by Dyer Island on the sea side, travelling southeast towards Cape Agulhas. It was enough: the sharks that had cautiously started to return took fright and fled.

At the time Port and Starboard were over 200 miles away, and the transiting pod of Orcas was probably no threat, but the mere presence of the Killer whales was enough to trigger a fresh exodus.

Wilfred Chivell and Brian McFarlane have a lot in common. Both had been diamond divers, wreck divers, spearfishermen, and now they owned and ran Shark Town's two largest cage-diving operators, Marine Dynamics and Great White Shark Tours respectively. They had the biggest boats, employed the most people and when, towards the end of January, they bumped into each other in the Blue Goose restaurant in Gansbaai, their conversation was predictable. Leaching money every day is neither pleasant nor sustainable, and although they were both on a stronger financial footing than the smaller operators, they both admitted that if the sharks did not return soon, the amber financial-warning lights would change to red.

The Blue Goose is one of Gansbaai's leading restaurants.

They were both aware of the various theories being considered to explain the disappearance of the sharks. One concerned an American researcher working with an operator known as Sharklady (Kim Maclean), who was experimenting with ultrasonic sound waves in the water – maybe this had driven the sharks away? A change in water temperature and oxygen levels was also being mooted, as was the possibility of poachers targeting the sharks. The poacher theory was supported by unconfirmed reports of two Great White carcasses having washed up near Cape Agulhas. A later twist to the poaching theory was a rumour – which was never substantiated – that the sharks were being fed explosive power heads to kill them primarily for their fins and teeth. Speculation, theories and flights of fancy were not the style of either man, but as they parted company to rejoin their respective tables, they agreed that a prayer or two might be a good idea.

Between 27th January and 4th February there were sporadic sightings, and with every day that sharks were seen, confidence in the industry grew. Then from 5th February to the 10th none of the boats reported seeing Great Whites. For five days from 10th February sightings were good, and improving every day. Then, just as Shark Town was breathing a huge sigh of relief, the weather turned bad and no-one could get to sea for six days.

By the end of February, though, life in Gansbaai was nearly back to normal, and all eight boats were doing as many trips daily as possible. By the middle of March the bad memories were fading and Shark Towners were beginning to believe the six-week rollercoaster had been an inexplicable, one-off event; the enigma of why the sharks had disappeared so comprehensively, only to reappear again, remained unsolved.

Translated into English, Gansbaai means 'Goose Bay'. For Shark Town, the Goose had reliably been laying golden eggs for 20 years, and everyone had prospered. The possibility that the bay's goose was growing tired and unreliable was something no-one really wanted to acknowledge – but not everyone bought the 'one-off' theory.

CHAPTER 7

Uncertain times

When the sharks reappeared, life in Shark Town
slowly started returning to normal. But the recent
absence of the Great Whites had sent shivers down
the spines of everyone in Shark Town; decades of
security had given way to an insecure future.

Dave Caravias

Some operators started to consider offering experiences
with other species present in local waters.

Wilfred Chivell was no stranger to setbacks in his career and had previously been brought down by financial circumstances beyond his control. Now, unbeknown to him, two Killer whales loomed ominously over his latest venture: would Port and Starboard prove to be equally destructive?

Wilfred remembered what it was like to 'go under', watching helplessly as events took over, and now he saw the folly in believing too readily that the shark hiatus had been a one-off event. He started planning against a recurrence – putting a new financial plan into place that would bolster his reserves in case the sharks disappeared again. Being the largest operator meant that he had the most to lose; on the other hand, he had more resources, and so more options.

Wilfred and his colleagues began examining and evaluating diversification options that could be put into action if the sharks disappeared again for a sustained period, impacting on the daily cash flow of Marine Dynamics. He had kept his regular Dyer Island Cruises running alongside Marine Dynamics and cage diving, and had set up an ongoing student/overseas volunteer programme. These companies, together with the Great White House restaurant, the curio shop and his non-profit organisations – the Dyer Island Conservation Trust and the African Penguin & Seabird Sanctuary – employed over 80 people, and provided a more diverse raft of opportunities for keeping people employed.

The responsibility sat heavily on Wilfred's shoulders, but it also provided an incentive to plan for a future in a world where things suddenly looked a lot less certain. He now needed to consider building up a reserve fund from which he could pay his staff and meet other costs for several weeks during a period of depleted income. Whale watching, bird watching, trips to see the penguin colony, and excursions out to sea looking for other species such as Blue and Mako sharks were all possibilities for which he now made plans, ready to be put into action if and when required.

Many of Marine Dynamics' visitors come specifically to see Great Whites, but lots of them could be equally interested in other shark species if they knew they were there. And although Gansbaai styled itself the

'Great White shark capital of the world', why not drop the 'Great White' and sell it as the 'Shark capital of the world'? Blues, Makos, Hammerheads, Bronze Whalers, Soupfin sharks, and others were all present in local waters at certain times of the year, as well as sawfishes and several species of ray. Whether they were shark divers, whale watchers or birders, most had an interest in wildlife in general, and Wilfred felt he had plenty to show them.

Marine volunteer programmes could be expanded, and internships offered. Wilfred immediately set about developing this initiative: he established the Marine Dynamics Academy, offering skills-based internships for marine biology students, with marine guiding and naturalist courses on offer. He would make sure that all engines, vehicles and equipment were serviced and maintained to the highest standards; this way he would be less likely to get hit with unexpected and expensive repair costs, such as for engine failure, or the need for unplanned equipment replacement.

As the weeks went by, Wilfred's and the town's confidence grew, and by the time the boom period of the December 2016 holiday season came, the Marine Dynamics team had many more options to offer than just a single shark species.

Dave Caravias had staggered financially through the six sharkless weeks. With fewer visitors, there was less for the staff at the Roundhouse to do. His wages bill had been self-regulating because the numbers of guests dictated the number of hours his staff worked, which in turn dictated what he paid them.

He had been generous and was proud that he had managed to keep all his staff employed through a difficult period. Like Wilfred Chivell, he had seen the writing on the wall and begun planning other ways of attracting guests. He would never again assume he could fill the Roundhouse by relying solely on Great White cage diving. With **Sharkbookings.com** he started promoting other shark ecotourism opportunities. To diversify his customer base for the Roundhouse, he kept trying new ideas; some worked, and some didn't. He ran kayak trips during the whale season, bought a safari vehicle and took guests to the top of the nearby mountains for wildlife viewing and sundowners, promoted sea trips to see other shark species, and started doing fatbike trips. These, in particular, were popular, something Dave attributes largely to the outstanding natural features of the area such as the inviting sand dunes.

As well as increasing guesthouse numbers, he took on managing the lettings of three self-catering houses. Before the six-week on-off shark-industry disruption, 95 per cent of Dave's guesthouse client base was Great White oriented. After the hiatus, Dave, like Wilfred, realised he needed more than one plan and as much diversification as possible if he was to survive in business.

Wilfred and Dave were not alone: there were many in Shark Town, including Brian Macfarlane and other operators, who realised that the future of their businesses, and indeed of the whole town's prosperity, relied on developing other features to attract visitors alongside Great Whites. They all took steps to bolster their cash reserves against the next shark rainy day. If Gansbaai had sidestepped the title of 'one-horse town' only to be called a 'one-shark town', things would have to change.

Resident shark scientist Alison Towner shared the financial concerns of the whole town, but there was also another dimension to her thinking. She had become a scientist for two reasons: one was her love of sharks, especially Great Whites, and the other was a compulsion to find answers, to solve mysteries. Now something had happened in the ocean that she didn't understand, and the scientist in Alison was excited at the prospect of solving a new mystery.

Many theories were being discussed to explain the near total disappearance of the sharks. Alison didn't believe that any one of them provided the full picture, although maybe a combination of factors, such as water-temperature and oxygen-level changes, acoustic experiments and poaching, could account for the exodus. But still she didn't think so. There was something missing from the argument. She talked to fellow marine biologist Alison Kock about Orcas being plausible predators of the Sevengill sharks in False Bay; although there was no actual proof, the possibility that Dyer Island's sharks had also been preyed on by Orcas started to gain traction in her mind.

Reports existed of Great White sharks having previously disappeared from an area when faced with localised threats. In 2012 a United States-based research operation called Ocearch had conducted large-scale operations catching and tagging Great Whites in False Bay, Gansbaai and Mossel Bay, and in each case the sharks had fled. It had then taken some weeks after the research vessel left before the sharks returned in normal numbers. If Alison Kock was right, and Orcas had been preying on the Sevengill sharks in False Bay, why couldn't they also have been attacking Gansbaai's sharks?

There was, however, a problem with this theory: Orcas had been seen in False Bay but not around Dyer Island. Nevertheless, Alison Towner was excited; she felt she was in the right place at the right time and might be participating in resolving a puzzle of nature. On a practical level, she needed her job in order to pay her rent, which could be threatened if the sharks left again. The flipside was that she needed data and would only get it, and start being able to solve the disappearance scientifically, if the sharks disappeared again – Alison was stuck in a classic Catch 22 dilemma! But despite these tensions, she felt that she had embarked on an adventure that would be life changing.

Out of sight is often out of mind, and as 2016 wore on, memories of the earlier absence of the sharks started fading. The people of Shark Town were working flat out catering for an influx of tourists, and the cage-diving industry recouped losses and had a very successful 2016/2017 Christmas holiday season. By early 2017 the events that had evoked

Gansbaai's busy main street showed a return to high visitor numbers during the Christmas holiday season of 2016/2017, and saw earlier losses recouped.

Richard Peirce

fear and doubt in Shark Town early the previous year were regarded as mere blips, a one-off series of events that wouldn't happen again, and a memory that many people chose to forget. No-one could have predicted the dramatic events that would occur as 2017 wore on, when Shark Town would again stare ruin in the face. It would still be a while before an unlikely saviour made its appearance.

On 17th January 2017 there were confirmed sightings of Port and Starboard off Langebaan on South Africa's west coast. From there they travelled south and were seen off Cape Town on 5th February. The January and early February sightings indicated they were heading back towards Gansbaai. But when they were sighted near Dyer Island on 7th February, it was the first time they were actually confirmed as being present in the area.

CHAPTER 8

The bad dream returns

All was going well again in the cage-diving
capital of South Africa – or was it? Business owners
and workers were now edgy: listening to news,
evaluating the changing situation and trying to stay
calm. Hope and despondency vied with each other,
turning as often and as quickly as the tide.

Mist often obscured views at sea and now prospects
for the future were obscured too – by uncertainty.

Sarah Munro-Kennedy

The sea mist still clung on stubbornly in patches between the mainland and Dyer Island on the morning of 7th February 2017. It was overcast and there was no wind, so the mist was able to linger longer than on other days when wind and sun would have cleared it earlier.

Most of the boats did two early trips and encountered lots of sharks. Those on board Marine Dynamics' boat *Slashfin* were treated to special sightings: eight different sharks were recorded on the first trip, and on the second trip the first shark encountered was a well-known male called Sellendilloh. This large male still had a spot tag attached to its dorsal fin, which had been placed there by the Ocearch team in 2012. The largest shark seen on the second trip was a 4.2-metre female, which contrasted sharply with a juvenile male of half her size that the enthusiasts on board had seen just before her.

At the end of the second trip, on their way back to Kleinbaai, *Slashfin* cruised down Shark Alley between Dyer Island and Geyser Rock to give the visitors a close-up view of the huge Cape fur seal colony. Back at the harbour the visitors filed off the boat and up the hill, talking excitedly about their amazing experiences. Gansbaai was living up to its reputation as the 'Great White shark capital of the world', and none of the visitors on any of the boats that went cage diving that day would have disputed the claim.

In the early afternoon Alison Towner was on her balcony looking out to sea, towards the southwest. It was a familiar view, but one of which she never tired. The clouds and the sun fought their endless battle, and the sea changed colour as it reacted to whichever one was winning. Alison was trying to decide whether, when the temperature cooled that evening, to go for a run, when her cell phone buzzed noisily and demanded attention. Her friend Grant was a skipper who worked for an operator called White Shark Projects: he had just sighted Port and Starboard cruising along towards Dyer Island.

The view of the bay from
Alison Towner's window.

Skipper Hennie Otto.

Alison felt both fear and excitement as the adrenaline coursed through her body. She set off for the Marine Dynamics office, calling in from her car on the way. But news travels fast, and by the time she got there, skipper Hennie Otto and others were already preparing to launch *Slashfin* to go and look for the two Orcas. The boat easily caught up with the pair, although they were moving quite fast in a southwesterly direction towards Danger Point. For the first time, footage and photos proving the presence of the two Killer whales in the vicinity of Dyer Island was captured on both still and video cameras.

The tall, almost scythe-like dorsal fins of Orcas usually make them easy to see and to track on the surface. Port and Starboard's collapsed fins, however, made it far more challenging to keep them in sight. With all eyes on board straining, and arms waving, skipper Hennie Otto struggled with the familiar compromise of getting as close to the animals as he could without endangering or crowding them.

For the first time Port and Starboard were recorded in the area on camera.

Their distinctive collapsed dorsal fins made Port and Starboard easy to identify.

The Orcas' behaviour was erratic. They would swim together side by side, then head off in different directions before diving and disappearing, only to reappear again, swimming side by side. They would hug the coastline for a while, then suddenly head directly offshore. *Slashfin* followed the Killer whales for a couple of hours before turning home for Kleinbaai. The happy, smiling faces of the crew indicated that everyone thought they had had a fantastic experience. Some of those on board had never seen an Orca, and no-one realised the deadly significance of what they thought was just a rare, exciting and lucky wildlife encounter.

By the time Alison got home that evening she had given up any idea of going for a run, and instead took her dogs for a walk on the beach. As she walked, her mind was still out at sea, wondering where the two Killer whales were and what they were doing. She had her fears and suspicions but, at the same time, as a scientist, she was excited – was the puzzle of why the sharks had disappeared last year about to be solved?

Later that night, lying in bed long after the excitement of the day's sightings, her thoughts became troubled. If the disappearance of the sharks last year had indeed been due to the presence of Orcas, now that they were back, would the sharks disperse again? And if so, for how long? And what would be the effect on the Great White shark tourism industry and, ultimately, on hundreds of jobs and the lives they supported? At last she fell into a troubled sleep, not knowing whether to be excited or worried about what might be happening out at sea, and what tomorrow might bring.

Five kilometres away, Wilfred Chivell was also having trouble getting to sleep. He had been in Cape Town earlier when *Slashfin* had gone to sea in search of the Orcas, and had been fully briefed regarding the sighting and positive identification of Port and Starboard. He was aware of Alison Kock's research in False Bay, and the conclusions that were being drawn after the Sevengill sharks had been discovered lying dead on the seabed, with their livers removed. He knew that she was convinced that Orcas had been responsible,

Wilfred Chivell

For workaholics Wilfred Chivell and partner Susan, holidays are rare, and usually geared to viewing wildlife – here in the Milford Sound, New Zealand.

and that Alison Towner also tended towards this belief. If the presence of the Orcas near Gansbaai meant sharks would leave the area again, he was better prepared than he had been last time, but was he prepared enough?

The clock on his bedside table told him it was two in the morning. His partner was fast asleep beside him and he didn't want to wake her, so he slid out of bed and quietly crept to the kitchen to make a cup of coffee. He crossed to the window and stared out to sea. Never still, never the same from one minute to the next, the sea was an oily black mass, dimly lit by the stars and the moon when they found gaps in the clouds.

Wilfred's brow was furrowed as he sipped his coffee, and his mind echoed the thoughts that had occupied Alison as she had also struggled to sleep: where were the Orcas now, and what were they doing? Dawn on 8th February was now only hours away, and by the end of that day there would be the first clues in answer to the questions that had kept Wilfred and Alison awake.

The flat sea and slight swell that Wilfred had observed during the hours of darkness was still there as dawn broke. A slight wind from the southwest intermittently disturbed the surface and caused the occasional small white horse.

By the time *Slashfin* had anchored with her first group of shark enthusiasts that morning, the crew had already heard from other, earlier boats that they hadn't seen any sharks. On the short journey from Kleinbaai, those on board *Slashfin* had caught several glimpses of the two Killer whales with the collapsed fins. There had been only three sightings of Orcas in the area in the last four years, and the visitors on today's trip were talking about how lucky they had been.

The normal summer chumming sites near the beach did not produce any sharks, and some boats moved out to the islands where they usually worked in the winter. Most boats had blank trips but those aboard *Slashfin* were lucky because they were visited by small juvenile Great Whites on both trips that day.

By the end of the day on 8th February many of those involved in cage diving were aware that Port and Starboard had been sighted in the area. For some people faint alarm bells started ringing, but for most it would take a little longer before the significance of their presence became apparent.

We don't know whether Great Whites actually feel fear, or whether their reactions are based purely on instinct. But for most humans the idea that the 'deadly' Great White shark could flee in terror from any other sea creature would be difficult to believe. It would take the events of the coming days and weeks to underline the certain and terrible fate from which the Gansbaai Great Whites were compelled to flee.

Thursday 9th February would go down as a significant day in the history of Shark Town. Late in the morning the Dyer Island Conservation Trust got a phone call reporting that a dead Great White had been washed up at Pearly Beach. This is an area of strong currents and, in the past, two Whale sharks had been washed up at the same place.

Supervised by marine biologists Alison Towner and Kelly Baker, the Trust's staff and International Marine volunteers used their heavy-duty off-road vehicle to retrieve the 2.6-metre female shark. The young animal was intact and there were no immediately obvious signs of trauma. Back at the volunteers' lodge the sand was washed off and, with input on the phone from Dr Alison Kock, all markings were observed, measured and photographed and other data recorded.

Later in the day representatives from the Department of Environmental Affairs came and took the carcass away to conduct a necropsy (animal autopsy). For Alison and Kelly there had been no conclusive external evidence of the cause of death. Scratch marks around the head gave cause for suspicion, but before scientists give opinions they like facts and evidence. However, the washing up of the young Great White was the first day of 2017 on which none of Shark Town's boats reported seeing any sharks – and the scientists all recognised the coincidence.

The days that followed started with hope and finished with despondency and, increasingly, with outright despair. The sharks had gone again, bringing the shark drought of the previous year sharply back into focus.

Valentine's Day (14th February) was the sixth consecutive day without sharks. Anyone visiting the Great White House coffee shop in the middle of that afternoon would have seen three young women huddled around a corner table, nursing coffees. Scientists Alison Towner and Kelly Baker, together with their colleague Brenda du Toit, were airing their suspicions that Orca predation was the reason for the absence of sharks.

All markings were measured, photographed and recorded.

Mostly land based, Brenda du Toit savours the chances she gets to go to sea.

CHAPTER 9

Community matters

Many residents along the coast had earned their living
from the sea for generations. While they worried about
the new insecurity, they also remembered a past
tragedy that took their minds off present worries and
underlined the dangers of working at sea.

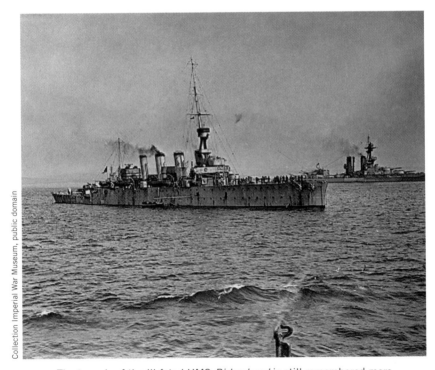

Collection Imperial War Museum, public domain

The tragedy of the ill-fated HMS *Birkenhead* is still remembered more
than 160 years after she sank off Danger Point near Gansbaai.

On 26th February 1852, HMS *Birkenhead* hit the rocks off Danger Point and sank. The ship has more than one claim to fame: as she foundered it was the first time the command 'women and children first' was heard. This command was part of the 'Birkenhead Drill', and, thanks to the command, no women and children died that day. Sadly, however, there was considerable other loss of life among the crew and the young soldiers aboard her.

Her second claim to fame is gold. The *Birkenhead* was reputed to be carrying 3 tonnes of gold stored secretly in her powder room. The value of gold goes up and down but, over time, has steadily increased. At the time of writing in late 2018, gold on international markets was worth about $2,000 an ounce. At this value, the fabled 'Birkenhead gold' would be worth some 65 million dollars today – a staggering sum of money. At various times divers have attempted to find the Birkenhead gold, but to this day it has not been discovered, and its existence remains an open question – and a tempting challenge for treasure hunters.

Sunday 26th February was Birkenhead Commemoration Day. Marine Dynamics, Dyer Island Cruises and others launched their boats and headed to Birkenhead Rock for a wreath-laying ceremony. As *Slashfin* cut through the water on her way to the ceremony, Wilfred thought of lives lost and others saved and, as always, offered a silent prayer thanking God for his own life and health – and then swallowed a couple of times to clear the lump in his throat. This was never a happy day in the Shark Town calendar, and today worry and uncertainty were added to many people's feelings of sadness: this was the 18th day with no sharks, and tourist activity had all but stopped.

Chivell, Brian MacFarlane, Dave Caravias and all the other diving operators, guesthouse, restaurant and gift shop owners, and many others – both employers and employees – were back in the same sharkless nightmare of a year ago. In 2016 no-one had understood why the sharks had disappeared, and assorted theories had done the rounds. This time, although there was still no hard evidence, there was only one theory – that the Great Whites had met more than their match: Orcas.

On the evening of 3rd March there was a buzz in Kleinbaai and Gansbaai. Fishermen had reported seeing Great Whites back in the area. The next day, four of the boats went out in search of sharks. Long before the first vessel had returned, ship-to-shore radios had conveyed the news to Christina Rutzen in her harbour master's office, and although the day was overcast, for her, the sun had come out. On the water the crews were happy and relieved and the visiting cage divers all realised how lucky they were. Cell phones were ringing on the boats and on land, and by lunchtime the news was all over Shark Town – the Great Whites were back!

There were no confirmed sightings of Port and Starboard for the rest of March, and shark numbers recovered. And once again human memories proved short as the bad times quickly receded. At the same time, there was a subtle but important change of attitude in the community. Those in the cage-diving industry often said how lucky they were to be where they were, doing what they were doing. Sometimes it was heartfelt, but often it was only half meant. The sharks had been seen as a permanent feature, and for 20 years their almost continuous presence had been taken for granted. The subtle change in attitude was that now, when people said they were lucky, they really meant it – and hoped that luck would stay with them.

Two very different and, it could be argued, contradictory events occurred in mid-April 2017. On the 15th an artwork called 'Kings of the Sea' was unveiled in a dominant position in Kleinbaai harbour, facing out to sea towards Dyer Island. The artwork, created by Jenna Harris, had been commissioned by Wilfred Chivell and was unveiled by Dudley Coetzee, the Deputy Mayor of the Overstrand. Jenna Harris is passionate about the ocean and its creatures. Not only had she created the artwork for Chivell, she had also written the epigram on the accompanying plaque, which reads: 'Mindful of these great white soldiers, I can hear the ocean's plight. This, one of the last safe havens, A kingdom of light.' The piece was Chivell's way of thanking and honouring the Great White fish that many consider to be the 'King of the Seas'.

Almost as if to denigrate this celebration of the Great White and to showcase their power, Port and Starboard reappeared in the area a few days later, and confirmed sightings were listed on the 19th and 30th April, with an unconfirmed report on the 28th. They were back, and their return triggered the most dramatic events yet in the battle between the two super-predators.

On land, Jenna Harris' artwork pays tribute to the 'Kings of the Sea' – the Great White sharks; while at sea, the Orcas call such claims into question.

CHAPTER 10

Proof!

Since the Great Whites had first disappeared,
multiple theories had arisen to explain their absence.
What had caused the sharks to flee? It would not
be long before evidence presented itself, allowing
scientists to reach firm conclusions.

Hennie Otto

Eventually the sea delivered up telling evidence.

Not long after daybreak on 3rd May, a Gansbaai resident fisherman and his wife were walking on Franskraal beach to the east of Kleinbaai, when they spotted something very large washing up in the surf. Being a fisherman, he was immediately able to identify the huge, almost 5-metre-long creature as a Great White shark, which was clearly dead. By soon after 7 a.m. the Dyer Island Conservation Trust (DICT) had been alerted and shark specialists Alison Towner and Kelly Baker and a team of Marine Dynamics' volunteers were on their way to retrieve the carcass with their heavy off-road vehicle and specialist equipment.

The shark was female, and her huge size was underlined when she was loaded onto the vehicle: she was so long that her entire head hung out over the back of the flatbed. Alison followed the truck as the shark was taken to where she would be thoroughly examined. She watched the head doing its dance of death as the vehicle bumped along, and feelings of sadness competed with her excitement. She was keen to begin the necropsy, but this was a breeding-age female belonging to a threatened species, and exciting though the science would be, she wished the shark could still have been alive and swimming in the ocean.

The Department of Environmental Affairs gave permission for the dissection to be carried out on site, supervised by Dr Malcolm Smale, who

Alison Towner examines a washed-up carcass.

flew in from Port Elizabeth to oversee the necropsy on 4th May. Even before the dissection started, Alison and Kelly began to suspect that they knew this shark. They were both avid watchers of *Game of Thrones*, and had named one of the female sharks they saw regularly 'Khaleesi', after a lead character in the series. Their suspicions were later confirmed – adding another dimension of sadness to the grim drama that was unfolding. Dr Smale was assisted by Dr Alison Kock, Alison Towner, Kelly Baker and others. It was soon evident that the shark's entire liver was missing, removed through a large, gaping hole on her underside. Sharks' livers contain an oil called squalene, which is lighter than water; so once the opening was made, the oil-rich liver would probably simply have popped out.

This was the largest Great White ever dissected in South Africa. All the data would have to be studied and the report finalised, but the experts were certain this was the work of Killer whales.

Dr Malcolm Smale with Alison Towner.

While the team worked at their grisly task, the next episode was unfolding at Franskraal beach, where another shark was found at 5 p.m. This time it was a 3.5-metre male, which was in a much more degraded state than Khaleesi had been. A tired team of scientists went to bed on 4th May, knowing they would have to carry out another dissection the following day. Those two days, 4th and 5th May 2017, would be forever imprinted on the minds of those involved in Gansbaai's shark cage-diving industry. The findings of the autopsy on the male shark were similar to those relating to Khaleesi. Its entire liver was missing, as well as its testes and heart, and even though it was in a more degraded state, a very similar liver exit wound was noted. Two dead sharks on land and no live sharks in the sea. The first two bodies were grim harbingers of what was to follow.

Late in the morning of 7th May, Dr Alison Kock received an unwelcome phone call from the local NSRI site manager. Another dead Great White had washed up at Struisbaai, near Cape Agulhas and 83 kilometres along the coast to the east of Gansbaai.

The Dyer Island Conservation Trust (DICT) team were the closest and so they took charge of retrieving the latest carcass. The retrieval had a messy start because, although the shark was complete, its stomach was outside the body cavity. This meant that it had to be detached before the shark could be loaded and transported. The dirty job of cutting the stomach free and examining its contents fell to marine biologist Alison Towner who, together with Kelly Baker and their colleagues, had arrived in Struisbaai to put their recently honed retrieval skills into action again. By now Alison had developed her own bomb-proof stomach, immune to the nauseating smells emanating from dead sharks.

They followed the same comprehensive protocol used by Dr Smale and took extensive samples and measurements. And this time, the work took six hours to complete. Once again, the wound was under the left pectoral fin, and once again the entire liver was missing, although, unlike

Necropsies (animal autopsies) are dirty and smelly procedures, and even more so with partly decomposed bodies, but the data gathered is of huge value to science.

(DICT = Dyer Island Conservation Trust)

the previous male, this time the heart and testes were still present. His stomach contained remnants of Cape fur seals and shark vertebrae, and a stingray barb was found embedded in his jaw.

'We have never seen anything like this. Today's carcass is another large Great White shark; he is a 4.15-metre male and his injuries seem to match those found in the previous two dead specimens. It seems likely that Orcas are again the cause of death, but we will confirm this after the autopsy. Obviously, this is a very sad time for us all. Nature can be extraordinary and unpredictable and the dexterity these enormous animals are capable of is mind-blowing. It is almost surgical precision as they remove the squalene-rich liver, and then leave or dump the carcass.' Towner made her comments in the Marine Dynamics Blog on 8th May, having completed this third necropsy.

Kelly Baker identified all three dead sharks from the DICT photo ID database. They had all been regular visitors to the Dyer Island area. The larger male had fully calcified claspers (reproductive organs) which, together with his size, indicated sexual maturity. Two of the three victims had been breeding-age animals. How many other Great White carcasses might still be on the seabed or have washed further out into the ocean? The population dynamic of southern African Great Whites, and the size of the population, were prime study areas for Alison Towner. Population estimates varied, but all agreed that Great Whites are a threatened species. She now knew of the certain loss of two breeding-age animals. She suspected there could be many more, and wondered what the impact would be on the future of Great White sharks on South Africa's coast.

For Wilfred Chivell, conservation of wild fauna and flora and scientific knowledge of the natural world are priorities. There wouldn't be eco-tourism without wildlife, and there wouldn't be wildlife without conservation and science, the two activities going hand in glove.

Three carcass retrievals had required the deployment of extensive resources and cost a lot of money. A considerable amount of the money generated by Marine Dynamics, Dyer Island Cruises and Wilfred's restaurant and shop was used to help fund the science and conservation work carried out by the Dyer Island Conservation Trust, and far too few people gave credit to Wilfred for having paid all the costs for all three retrievals and the investigations that followed.

By the time the third shark washed ashore on 8th May, Shark Town had already had a sharkless week. Following the discovery of the three dead sharks a depressing gloom settled on the town like a heavy blanket. Boats went to sea each day, either taking out expectant shark fans, or just doing a little chumming in the hope of finding that the sharks were back.

On Sunday 14th May there were five boats at anchor chumming for sharks. There was only a slight wind, the sun had few clouds to hide behind, and the sea was calm. The vessels all seemed connected by an invisible cord of nervous depression. Suddenly the cord snapped and, with uncanny co-ordination, everyone looked the same way at the boat nearest the beach. Everyone on board was staring into the water, watching the familiar shadow of a large shark.

It was strange: there were no whoops of joy, and almost no talking, as a collective sigh of relief relinked the vessels and dispelled the remains of the earlier gloom. The next day saw all the boats out, and a week of shark sightings followed until, on the 20th, a red tide algal bloom seemed to slow down shark action. The red tide took some days to clear, and then a cold front arrived and brought with it large numbers of sharks.

May turned into June and, as each day rolled by, confidence grew, but no-one took the presence of Great Whites for granted any more. Every day brought sighs of relief as the first sharks were seen, and the boat crews said silent prayers of thanks.

Shark Town was now adjusting to a new reality. As long as Port and Starboard stalked South Africa's coasts, and visited the Dyer Island area, Shark Town's Great Whites would come and go as they, too, adjusted to the new dynamic of regular visits from a superior apex predator.

Southern Right whales, such as these seen
off the southern Cape coast, and Great
White sharks are the main attractions
bringing marine ecotourists to the area.

Sandra Hoerbst

Wilfred Chivell, Brian MacFarlane, Dave Caravias, Christina Rutzen and others got used to the ups and downs as reliable, almost daily Great White sightings started to be a wish rather than a safe expectation. The words 'Port' and 'Starboard' were now spoken in fear, and among Shark Towners there were those who wanted them removed. Discussions were held about how the two Killer whales could be tagged so that they could be tracked, caught and removed, or even blown up!

The two Killer whales could reappear at any time, and not knowing where they were or when they would return was a constant niggle in the back of everyone's minds.

Port and Starboard were, of course, unaware of the intense human interest in their whereabouts, or of the serious effect their predation was having on South Africa's fragile population of Great Whites, and the marine ecology of the area. They were also unaware that there were many people who would happily have thrown sticks of dynamite at them.

In mid-June they crossed False Bay, then Betty's and Walker bays on their familiar cruise route heading for Dyer Island. The relative calm of late May and early June in Shark Town was about to be shattered.

Sunday 18th June was a brilliant day in every way. There was a slight swell, a cloudless sky, the wind was light but changeable, and there were sharks everywhere. The Marine Dynamics boat *Slashfin* did three trips to the Joubertsdam reef area and recorded six sharks on each of the first two trips, and five on the third one.

The slight chill in the air was hardly noticed by any of the operators because, like those on *Slashfin*, they all had plenty of sharks around their cages. Sunday's changeable wind increased, and on Monday and Tuesday all the boats were forced to stay ashore. What no-one on shore knew was that, while the boats were on their trailers on land, and Sunday's divers were still enthusing about their fantastic day out at sea, the silent killers had returned.

Everyone went back to sea on Wednesday 21st June with high expectations, but returned with their hopes having been dashed. All the boats recorded a blank: the Great Whites had gone again.

Bad weather returned on Wednesday night, forcing the boats ashore until Saturday 24th June, which turned out to be a repeat of shark-free Wednesday. But with one major difference – this time, Port and Starboard were seen in the area and positively identified. When Wilfred took a call early on Saturday morning he hadn't yet heard that the two Orcas were back in the area: but another Great White, number four, had been found washed up.

Wilfred, Alison Towner, skipper Hennie Otto and others met on Pearly Beach and stared in silence at the ghostly pale, semi-decomposed body of the 4.1-metre male shark. Alison, by now experienced in Great White necropsies, observed that sharks that had had their livers removed were always much lighter in colour than normal, probably because of the resulting massive blood loss.

Teams from Marine Dynamics and DICT swung into action and retrieved the shark. The necropsy told the same story as for the previous three, the carcass manifesting the now familiar gaping wound under the pectoral fin and the missing liver.

The nightmare was back.

Although no-one realised it at the time, Sunday 18th June 2017 would mark the beginning of the longest period without sharks that Gansbaai had experienced so far. On 14th July a single female Great White was sighted, but apart from this there were to be 48 days without Great Whites. For the hundreds of people in Shark Town and the surrounding area who relied on the industry, concern turned to worry, to despair and then to hopelessness.

Wilfred, Brian, Dave and others were in the front line. They were the employers, they had the responsibility and they felt it keenly. As the days went by, the spectre that soon staff would have to be laid off haunted everyone. Firing staff for not doing their job properly, because they annoyed you, or because they had committed a misdemeanour was unpleasant but relatively easy. But letting staff go whom you knew and liked, who did their jobs well and who had families to support, was beyond difficult – it was heart-breaking.

Business owners strategised and hoped. They put their various plans B and C into operation and watched their reserves dwindle. Harbour master Christina Rutzen was at the centre of the despair. She saw the disappointment on the faces of the crews and the visitors as, day after day, they came back reporting no sightings of Great Whites. Her husband Frank, a skipper working for Supreme Sharks, was an early casualty when the company was forced to fold as a result of the new sharkless order.

All over Shark Town the various support businesses were also feeling the pinch, and Dave Caravias watched the number of his guesthouse visitors drop dramatically. At the beginning of the Great White drought, many operators followed their normal policy of offering free return trips. Brian MacFarlane was so confident of an imminent upturn that he initially gave 100 per cent refunds; when this proved unaffordable, he reduced the refund to 50 per cent, before he and Wilfred both agreed to give 25 per cent refunds when sharks were not seen. Operators tried various refund and return-trip options before many simply shut their doors and started waiting for the sharks to come back. The whole of the community was stranded. For most it was a test of endurance: would their money last until the sharks came back, or would doors close permanently, and jobs be lost forever?

Most of Dave Caravias' guests in the Roundhouse had come to see Great Whites, and even more people visited his **www.sharkbookings.com** website, enquiring about where else they could dive with the king of sharks. For the last half of June and the whole of July, Dave became a shuttle driver, taking guests almost daily either to Mossel Bay or False Bay

Dolphin sightings were particularly welcome when sharks were in short supply.

in pursuit of sharks. Because, while Gansbaai was experiencing a Great White drought, Mossel Bay's operators reported seeing lots of sharks every day. In False Bay there were other options, and some divers were happy to go to the Simon's Town area to dive with Sevengill sharks. Dave wasn't alone in benefitting from sharks in other places and from the tourists desperate to see them. Taxi drivers from both Gansbaai and Hermanus got used to being asked to do long drives to Mossel Bay, where extra shark trips had to be organised.

Although visitors to Shark Town weren't seeing Great Whites, a small number of die-hard enthusiasts kept coming, and they were rewarded with some fantastic sightings. The whales and dolphins had appeared almost as if they were trying to help: Humpbacks, Brydes and Southern Right whales were regularly seen, and dolphins patrolling the coast were also often sighted in large numbers.

As July drew to a close, a few boats still set out each day, continuing to look for Great Whites. They went more in hope than in expectation. Christina Rutzen watched the comings and goings and wondered when and how it would all end. Then, in early August, an unexpected saviour appeared and threw a lifeline to Shark Town.

CHAPTER 11

Nature abhors a vacuum

After repeated reverses and recoveries in
the cage-diving industry, local businesses
had to plan for the new reality. The entrepreneurs
who had pioneered cage diving were thinking of
ways to diversify their business when nature
stepped in and provided much-needed help.

Bronze Whalers (aka Copper sharks) to the rescue.

On Thursday 3rd August 2017, as the shadow first approached Marine Dynamics' boat *Slashfin*, the tension was palpable; the Great Whites were back! However, as the shape became clearer, the colour and the distinctive rounded snout identified it as a Bronze Whaler – an impressive shark itself. This unexpected but very welcome new arrival was potentially a saviour for the beleaguered cage-diving industry. On both trips, visitors got into the cage and experienced a large shark close-up, and for the first time in 48 days, genuine 'sharky' grins lit up the visitors' faces.

The Marine Dynamics Blog for the day states 'Number of White sharks. O + O'. The blog then goes on to record that on both of their trips they had seen Bronze Whalers. These sharks are also known as Copper sharks or Narrowtoothed sharks, and that day several of the boats had cause to say thank you to what are locally known as Bronzies.

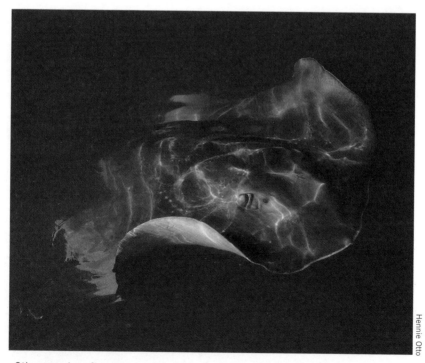

Hennie Otto

Stingrays also often appeared, helping the Copper sharks fill the Great White gap.

One operator commented that the Bronze Whalers had literally saved his industry.

Some shark fans were noticeably disappointed at not seeing Great Whites, but most, if they were disappointed, hid it well and were just grateful and happy that they had seen a large shark.

Then on Sunday 6th August, for the first time in many weeks, Great Whites were again present around the cages. And, as a bonus, the Bronze Whalers turned up as well! Monday was a red-letter day in Shark Town – the Great Whites were back in numbers, and all the boats reported very welcome sightings.

Having discovered the area being chummed, the Bronzies now became regular performers at the Dyer Island shark show. Stingrays also often appeared in the supporting cast, and these two species provided some insurance for when Great Whites did not appear. For the rest of August and the whole of September, Great Whites were present in good numbers and visitors got used to being spoilt by a reliable headliner and a supporting act as well.

But in spite of the good times, attitudes in Shark Town had changed with the new reality. The days of virtual guarantees of diving with Great Whites had gone. The operators were all completely open with their clients, and those who came to see Great Whites were just as grateful as the boat crews when sharks were in evidence.

A clear pattern was starting to emerge. Port and Starboard would arrive in the area and kill a few Great Whites, and the underwater equivalent of jungle drums would sound, sending the survivors fleeing for safety.

For some reason, the Bronze Whalers did not seem to be similarly affected at this time. Maybe they were not a target for the Orcas, or maybe they hadn't yet become targets. Whatever it was, the diving operators owed a great deal to the supporting act because it was this backup that kept the industry afloat.

Before Port and Starboard became major influences in the marine ecology in the Dyer Island area and the Great Whites started having to flee from predators, Bronze Whalers had not been present in large numbers in the adjacent Kleinbaai area. Until then, these sharks had usually been caught by local fishermen in Walker Bay during October and November.

It wasn't too long after the Bronze Whalers had first started appearing regularly that opportunism came into the story, and provided a bizarre new threat. Local fishermen had noted the presence of the Bronzies and realised they could catch them and turn a profit. They set about hooking and catching them, often right in front of the tourist boats that were putting people in the water to dive with those very sharks. Not only were the tourists horrified watching the sharks being caught and killed in front of them, but the cage-diving industry was now at loggerheads with local fishermen. Wilfred Chivell stepped in to try to stop the slaughter. Attempts to persuade the fishermen and appeal to their better natures failed, which left money to do the talking: the only option was to try to buy off the fishermen.

A dead Bronze Whaler was worth about R1,000, or R7 per kilogram to the fishermen. Australia was a historic export market for these sharks, and more recently they have been sold for human consumption in Africa as a cheap source of protein. The fins of most sharks caught in South Africa, including those of Bronze Whalers, are exported to China and the Far East. So these sharks are worth catching even though they are not particularly valuable.

Walker Bay fishermen would catch five or six Bronzies a night, and while the size of the new but transient Kleinbaai area population was not accurately known, it was estimated that 50 to 70 individuals were being seen. Given that the cage-diving industry had come to need the insurance provided by Bronzies, their live value to tourism far exceeded their relatively modest dead value to the fishermen. Some of the operators, led by Wilfred and including Brian McFarlane, started compensating the fishermen for *not* catching Bronze Whalers. The strategy worked, but it would only be sustainable as long as compensation payments were reasonable.

On 2nd October, Port and Starboard were sighted near Danger Point, close to Gansbaai. The dive boats went to sea that day and although they did see Great Whites, sightings were few and intermittent. Bad weather kept the boats ashore for the next two days, and during this time the pattern repeated itself: the marine jungle drums warned of Orcas present and prompted the familiar exodus, so when the boats went back to chum for sharks on 5th October, they found Bronze Whalers but no Great Whites.

By 6th October the Orcas had moved on to False Bay and on the 9th and 10th, the Great Whites were starting to creep back to Gansbaai. Then the Orcas returned to Dyer Island on 11th October and history repeated itself.

Although the Great White was the focus of interest for most visitors, the irony was that, in many ways, the Bronze Whalers put on a better show. These smaller sharks were more reactive around the bait, often opened their mouths close to the cage, showed off an impressive array of shark teeth, and generally – in shark-operator parlance – 'worked better'. For the remaining months of 2017 Great Whites were present off and on; so were the Bronze Whalers, and stingray sightings seemed to be on the increase.

Sharks disappearing, Great White bodies washing up, and the culprits being fingered had all made 2017 a year that no-one in Shark Town would forget. The new certainty was that nothing was certain any more. People's attitudes adjusted, businesses adjusted, and the marine ecosystem adjusted.

Frustrating and frightening though the situation was for the ecotourism sector, it was exciting from a marine ecological perspective. The patterns and rhythms of life in the ocean were changing and evolving. For naturalists, scientists and specialist marine ecologists, the actions of Port and Starboard were producing fascinating new realities.

CHAPTER 12

2018 – a changed world

Recent times had been hard on the cage-diving
industry, but as more became known about the
Orca-vs-Great White saga, nuances crept in.
Was it 'all or nothing', or was there some wiggle
room in which businesses could operate? Could other
areas along the coast be explored, and other aspects
of life at Africa's southernmost tip be developed for
tourism? Adaptation would define the way forward.

Chris Fallows

The famous flying sharks – in some areas, Great Whites often leap
clear of the water (known as breaching) when hunting seals.

In November 2018 Dave Caravias commented: 'There were times this year when it felt as if we were being hit on all sides. Our sharks were not as reliable as they had been in the past, and visitors knew this, so numbers were often affected. In the beginning of the year the news went all over the world that Cape Town was about to run out of water, and then from March onwards violent demonstrations and riots started happening in the area. Who wants to come on holiday to a place where they might see no sharks, can't have a shower, and might get caught in a riot!?' His points were undeniably valid: Gansbaai's new world had its ups and downs. But for many in the shark industry there now seemed to be more downs than ups.

The dips in the fortunes of cage-diving operators had produced casualties all across Shark Town's ecotourism-reliant businesses. Frank Rutzen's employers, Supreme Sharks, had been forced to close. Among other losers were a cleaning firm and the Kleinbaai harbour clothing shop. Several staff members working in the industry had to be laid off. Many of the businesses that survived did so through a mix of shedding staff, temporary closures, and cutting costs wherever possible.

A chart (see pages 110–111) compiled by Simon's Town-based naturalist Dave Hurwitz shows the confirmed sightings of Port and Starboard. During 2018 the chart shows the presence of the two Killer whales along South Africa's south coast from Cape Town to Mossel Bay. The chart lists only confirmed sightings, and so is by no means a complete map of their movements. Additionally, although the distinctive collapsed dorsal fins of both whales made them easy to identify, it also made them less visible, which must certainly have impacted the number of sightings on the chart. Recorded sightings indicate that the Orcas travel huge distances and sometimes at very fast speeds.

The chart of 2018 starts with a sighting of the Orcas in January in Mossel Bay; in March they were again in Mossel Bay and also False Bay; in May, off Gansbaai and off Cape Town; then in July there are entries for

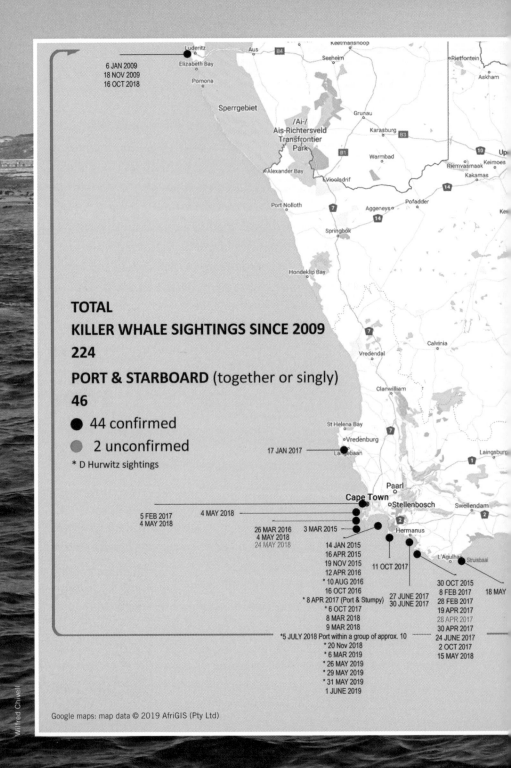

6 JAN 2009
18 NOV 2009
16 OCT 2018

TOTAL

KILLER WHALE SIGHTINGS SINCE 2009

224

PORT & STARBOARD (together or singly)

46

● 44 confirmed

● 2 unconfirmed

* D Hurwitz sightings

17 JAN 2017

5 FEB 2017
4 MAY 2018

4 MAY 2018

26 MAR 2016
4 MAY 2018
24 MAY 2018

3 MAR 2015

14 JAN 2015
16 APR 2015
19 NOV 2015
12 APR 2016
* 10 AUG 2016
16 OCT 2016
* 8 APR 2017 (Port & Stumpy)
* 6 OCT 2017
8 MAR 2018
9 MAR 2018
*5 JULY 2018 Port within a group of approx. 10
* 20 Nov 2018
* 6 MAR 2019
* 26 MAY 2019
* 29 MAY 2019
* 31 MAY 2019
1 JUNE 2019

11 OCT 2017

27 JUNE 2017
30 JUNE 2017

30 OCT 2015
8 FEB 2017
28 FEB 2017
19 APR 2017
28 APR 2017
30 APR 2017
24 JUNE 2017
2 OCT 2017
15 MAY 2018

18 MAY

Google maps: map data © 2019 AfriGIS (Pty Ltd)

KILLER WHALES
PORT & STARBOARD HISTORY
Sightings from: 6 January 2009 to 1 JUNE 2019

TIME AT SEA

DISTANCE: **970** nm   SPEED: | **5** | knots   DAYS AT SEA: **8.1**

Google Earth maps: map data © 2019 AfriGIS (Pty Ltd)

27 APRIL 2013
21 JULY 2018

24 JULY 2018

Dave Hurwitz's Killer whale sightings chart is constantly being updated with new sightings.

sightings off Plettenberg Bay and Port Elizabeth. By October they were in Namibia off Lüderitz, which, as far as current reports indicate, is the northern limit of their range.

The sightings chart broadly coincides with the appearance and disappearance of Great Whites off Gansbaai. No carcasses were washed up in 2018, which might indicate that the sharks were by then fully aware of the threat from Orcas, and were acting accordingly, somehow managing to evade the recently arrived, superior apex predators. The last entry on Hurwitz's chart, for 1st June 2019, is when, for the first time, the Orcas were seen predating on Cow sharks around Seal Island in False Bay.

In February 2017, at a time when Great Whites were completely absent from the usual chumming sites near Dyer Island, Dave Caravias had been out on a fatbike trip with clients near Die Plaat on the De Kelders (the northern) side of Walker Bay. He was coming down the 4x4 track near De Kelders when he saw a large shark close in to the beach. He messaged Alison Towner, who that day happened to be diving to check out various receivers she had placed on the seabed to track shark movements. Dave knew Alison was diving, and knew that she would be in the water very close to where he was watching the Great White shark. Alison got the message and aborted her dive. Dave and his group continued their ride, and from cliff tops they saw another two Great Whites swimming close in near the rocks.

Then, in 2018, a local luxury hotel called Grootbos started operating flights for guests around the picturesque coastline of Walker Bay. By this time Dave was often being hired by Grootbos to take their guests out on fatbike trips, and he got used to hearing reports from visitors of Great Whites seen from the air off De Kelders and outside the surf along the beach towards Hermanus. What Dave found curious was that sharks were being seen in many places other than around Dyer Island, where the cage-diving boats worked.

He wondered whether this indicated specific areas that the sharks avoided – or where they sought refuge – when the Orcas were around. Did the Orcas have preferred killing areas, or had the predations taken place around Dyer Island because that is where the most sharks are for most of the time?

Whatever the case, these sightings might mean that not all sharks flee far – some may move just out of the historic danger zone. The shark-diving operators have licences to chum for sharks in specific areas around Dyer

Dave's fatbike trips proved to be a great success.

Island and near the adjacent beach. If Dave's killing-zone theory proved correct, then drones could be used to search for sharks when they were absent from their usual areas. Although parts of Walker Bay are protected for the benefit of whales and other marine life (so even if sharks were known to be in these areas, it would not be possible for operators to go and look for them), were sharks discovered to be in other, unprotected areas, then operators could apply for variations to their permits. This could be one of the ways in which Shark Town's ecotourism would need to change in order to survive.

The Orca predations of the last two years now form part of Shark Town's global reputation. Chivell, McFarlane, Caravias and others are constantly on the lookout for new strings to their bows, knowing that the almost guaranteed daily Great White bonanza is over.

Dave Caravias

Cage-diving businesses will have to diversify, and maybe Great Whites will become just one of many attractions.

Kelly Baker

Bronze Whalers, the support act, often take star billing.

Five years ago, the idea of cage diving with Bronze Whalers would have been met with scepticism; now it is a reality for which everyone is grateful. Entrepreneurs are constantly on the lookout for new opportunities.

It probably won't be long before the Port and Starboard story itself is turned into a tourist attraction by some enterprising local business person. A shark museum, or an interactive shark centre, could take visitors on a journey through the history of Gansbaai's involvement with Great Whites. Starting with the liver-oil factory, going on to artisanal shark fisheries, through the development of cage diving, and finishing with the drama of the Orca predations threatening jobs and livelihoods, such a centre could quickly become a major local attraction.

The presence of Great Whites may now be uncertain, but what is certain is that Shark Town's human inhabitants are adapting to the new reality and will adapt further. Shark Town is situated in an area of outstanding natural beauty, and the waters off the coast are home to a wonderful abundance of marine species. The future may well see Great White sharks becoming just one of a bigger and better, wider and even more exhilarating range of attractions.

PART 2

CHAPTER 13

Orcas

In recent years films from *Free Willy* to *Blackfish* have brought Orcas to public attention all over the world, painting them as performers and fun figures. The new reality is that these ultimate ocean predators, these kings of the sea, are now under threat thanks to the impact of humans.

Hennie Otto

In Walker Bay there is both glee and despair when Orcas are sighted: glee on the part of tourists, and despair for locals.

Orcas have been present in our oceans for approximately 11 million years. With their starkly contrasting black-and-white coloration, their enormous, scythe-like dorsal fin and a fearsome reputation as the ocean's apex predators, they are the stuff of legends. Their name is thought to be derived from Orcus, a Roman god of the underworld. In times gone by, sailors observed Orcas attacking whales and called them 'whale killers'; over time, the words have become transposed, hence their alternative name, 'Killer whale'.

Orcas are found throughout the world's oceans and are generally accepted as being the most widespread mammal species after humans. Although they are most commonly recorded in temperate coastal waters, they also occur in the open ocean, cold waters, the tropics, and in enclosed and partially enclosed seas. They have even been known to enter estuaries, rivers and ice floes.

Orcas are the largest members of the dolphin family in a class of mammals called cetaceans, which comprises animals ranging from small harbour porpoises to the largest living creature on the planet, the Blue whale. Orcas are commonly referred to as 'whales' – the conventional term for any cetacean that generally attains a length of more than 4 metres. They have long been considered to be the only surviving species in the genus *Orcinus*, although there is now speculation that several discrete races, subspecies or even species may exist. So diverse are these mammals' 'habitats' that scientists have begun categorising them according to their preferred local environment, and there is an ongoing process of recording the distinctive physiological and dietary features of the various 'types', which can broadly be categorised as Resident, Transient and Offshore.

Female Orcas enjoy a lifespan of up to 100 years, while males die younger, at around 60 years. Male Orcas reach sexual maturity at about 15 years; females reach maturity in their early teens and reproduce every three to five years, from about their 15th year until about 50. Breeding can occur at any time of the year, although in the northern hemisphere births peak between October and March. Females give birth to single calves after a gestation period of 15 to 18 months. At birth, Orcas weigh, on average, 180 kilograms (400 pounds) and are 2.4 metres (8 feet) long. Calves double their body size in their first year of life.

Males are larger, and have larger dorsal fins, than females. This huge fin, which can measure up to 1.8 metres in height – taller than many humans – is the largest dorsal fin of all the cetaceans. The largest Killer whale ever caught was 9.75 metres (32 feet) long and weighed 9,979 kilograms (22,000 pounds).

Orcas have excellent sight and hearing, which they use for echolocation. Curiously, they do not have any olfactory capability: they have no organ for smelling, and no lobe of the brain dedicated to this function. Like other members of the dolphin family, Orcas never fall completely asleep because they have to keep surfacing in order to breathe. They are, however, able to 'half sleep' by shutting down half their brain at a time, while the other half takes care of their breathing; during such periods, they keep just one eye open at a time.

Sandra Hoerbst

Southern Right whale calves are on the Orca prey list. The tactic Orcas often use is to try to separate calves from their mothers – and then attack.

Orcas are carnivores, and they are thought to be the world's largest predators of warm-blooded animals. Seals, sea lions, dolphins, whales and sea otters are on the mammal prey list, and sharks, rays, squid, octopuses, fish, seabirds, sea turtles and others complete the menu. Populations in different places are often specialist feeders concentrating on hunting one particular prey species.

Scientific study has shown that Orcas are highly intelligent – possibly even more so than chimpanzees – and communicate widely, using a complex language that involves high-pitched whistles and screams, low-frequency pops and clicks, and pulsed calls; they also use physical antics involving touch, fin- or tail-slapping, breaching and head-butting. They have often been filmed hunting co-operatively, using complex strategies to secure their prey. Working together, they have been observed 'herding' fish and then stunning them using their tails. They pursue tuna and dolphins for long periods to tire them out; they then assemble a posse to

Dolphins belong to the same family as Orcas – but are nevertheless on the Orca prey list.

take on large whales; they also snatch seals, seabirds and other creatures resting on ice floes. Orcas have been observed temporarily stranding themselves on beaches to get at seals and sea lions. They often follow fishing vessels, having learnt that a meal will ensue when by-catch is discarded, and they have also worked out how to take prey caught on the hooks of baited longlines.

When attacking Southern Right whales, which then attempt to cluster together for better defence, Orcas have been observed trying to split up the group, or separate cows from their calves. Once they have killed such a whale, the Orcas usually eat only the tongue, apparently considered a delicacy.

Orcas' only predators are humans, who pose a threat by degrading and disturbing their ocean habitat, by inadvertently catching them on fishing expeditions, or by capturing them for commercial whaling or for exhibition in marine parks.

The film *Blackfish* was a factor in convincing SeaWorld
to abandon using Orcas in marine shows.

Orcas have a limited amount of recoverable oil, so they have never been particularly sought-after by whalers, although from 1935 until 1979, 26 were killed every year, on average. During the late 1970s/early 1980s Russian whaling ships killed over 900 animals in the southern hemisphere. South Africa was also involved, and between 1971 and 1975, 36 Killer whales were taken at the Durban whaling station.

Unfortunately for Orcas, their intelligence has attracted the attention of human entrepreneurs, who in the past century hunted them down and captured them for display in marine parks. During the years of their use in marine parks, over 150 Orcas died in captivity, at least 30 calves were stillborn, and 14 capture attempts resulted in Orcas dying. In August 2014 there were 52 Orcas held in captivity in eight countries; 28 of these were in the United States. Of the 52, 18 were captured from the wild and 34 were born and raised in captivity.

The *Free Willy* movie of 1993 triggered sympathy around the world for Orcas kept in captivity, where they were used as exhibits and taught to perform tricks in front of exhilarated crowds in marine parks across the world. The 2013 American documentary film *Blackfish* was a major catalyst in getting the SeaWorld chain to abandon the use of these animals in marine shows.

Their intelligence and sentience has caused them to suffer in captivity, and sometimes brought them into conflict with their handlers. Although there are no reports of Orcas deliberately attacking humans in the wild, there are several instances of attacks on humans by Orcas held in captivity; a captive whale called Tilikum killed three of his trainers – in 1991, 1999 and 2010.

But the historic threats to Orcas from limited commercial whaling or catching them for exhibits in marine parks may be insignificant compared to the insidious threat of PCBs or polychlorinated biphenyls, which are organic compounds that could push Orca populations to collapse, and lead to local extinctions. PCBs were once used in capacitors, marine oil paints, and coolants. They were discovered to be so dangerous that their manufacture was banned in the USA and other countries in the 1970s/1980s.

PCB levels in the environment have remained high even though their manufacture has stopped. This is partly because they are still found in what are called legacy products, such as cable insulation, some marine paints and transformers, and partly because they are long lived and break down slowly.

Toxins and ingested pollutants are found in the highest concentrations in animals at the top of the food chain. Orcas around the world have a widely variable diet and prey on animals that themselves have ingested PCBs, so the carcinogens build up in their blubber. Even now, Orcas across the northern hemisphere are among the most heavily contaminated animals on the planet.

One study looked at 19 northern hemisphere populations and found that 10 were in decline. The main cause of the decline was determined to be PCBs. Orcas living in seas near highly industrialised countries have been hardest hit. One pod, which mostly ranges up and down the west side of the British Isles, is now down to nine or ten individuals, and the pod has not produced a viable calf for some years.

PCBs are believed to be altering Orca behaviour, damaging their immune systems and harming reproduction to the extent that researchers suspect many families of Orcas may not survive the next few decades. The gravity of the PCB threat to Orcas is debated by scientists, but the existence of the threat is not.

Sadly, PCBs are by no means the only challenge these animals face. Whatever the challenge, be it PCBs, reduced fish stocks, climate change, pollution of one sort or another (including sound), or many others – humans are to some degree responsible.

No book featuring Port and Starboard would be complete without considering why the dorsal fins of some Orcas flop over. For many years it was thought that this condition affected only Orcas held in captivity. Clearly this is not the case, as is evidenced by Port and Starboard and many other recorded instances in the wild. Orcas' dorsal fins are supported by fibrous connective tissue called collagen. In captive animals, more males than females have collapsed fins, which is possibly because the fins on males are much larger.

Scientists from the National Marine Fisheries Service believe that the collapsed dorsal fin commonly seen in captive Orcas results not from a pathogenic condition, but rather because of a structural change in the collagen. In captive Orcas this could be the result of any one, or all, of the following: dietary changes, lowered blood pressure due to reduced activity, overheating of collagen due to overexposure to the ambient air, lack of water pressure support, being constrained to swim in circles, and dehydration of the collagen – and some of these factors could also affect wild animals. Furthermore, male Orcas can be aggressive towards one another, which can also cause damage to their fins. In South Africa it is not uncommon for fishermen to try to frighten Orcas away from threatening their catches by shooting or throwing thunder-flashes and other explosives at them – actions that could result in injury and damage to the dorsal fin. But in spite of all the conjecture, it seems that fin collapse in wild Orcas remains largely unexplained.

The degree of collapse in Port and Starboard's fins is almost identical. Assuming they have spent most of their lives together, they have probably been subjected to similar conditions and experiences, so whatever has caused the collapse in one could conceivably apply to the other. It may even be that their targeting of shark livers indicates a dietary deficiency that they are trying to correct. It can't be ruled out that Gansbaai's Great Whites are paying the price for this quest.

Port and Starboard have regularly been observed in the company of a pod of six Orcas that patrols South Africa's coasts. Some people hypothesise that this could be their 'family' pod, but that because of their damaged fins, they can't always keep up with the others, perhaps due to increased drag in the water. The Port and Starboard story is full of theories, and this is yet another one waiting for someone or something to prove or disprove it.

CHAPTER 14

Great White and Bronze Whaler sharks

The Great White shark has no known natural predators other than, occasionally, the Killer whale – and, more systematically, humans. Demonised in the movie *Jaws* (based on the novel by Peter Benchley), the Great White has been persecuted for its perceived danger towards humans, as well as overfished to the point that its conservation status is now Vulnerable on the IUCN list.

Hennie Otto

The film *Jaws* is often blamed for demonising sharks, and Great Whites in particular, but sharks have been feared by humans for centuries.

Reaching lengths of over 6 metres, and with large, slash-like gills, Great White sharks (scientifically identified as *Carcharodon carcharias*) are among the planet's most awe-inspiring creatures. There are records of very large Great Whites in the Mediterranean, and one theory is that the biblical tale about Jonah and the whale should perhaps more correctly be titled 'Jonah and the Great White Shark'. Great Whites generally inhabit the world's temperate seas. However, being semi-warm-blooded, they can to some extent regulate their body temperature, which increases their range into subtropical and even cold oceans.

Great White populations are seriously depleted as a result of overfishing, and they are now Red Listed by the International Union for the Conservation of Nature (IUCN) as Vulnerable. In spite of this they still exist in various hot spots, among which are off the coasts of South Australia, California and South Africa.

'Shark' has long been a word that sends shivers down human spines, and of all sharks, the Great White is the most feared (although Tiger and Bull sharks probably attack more people). In recent years shark advocates, conservationists and scientists have made strenuous efforts to persuade the world's public that their fear of sharks is largely irrational. These efforts have mostly been in vain: despite the facts, despite logic and statistics, the luridly sensational *Jaws*-type headlines persist, and the stereotypical image remains intact.

Why is it proving so difficult to change the way sharks are perceived? Great Whites are known to feed on seals, sea lions, cetaceans (small whales, dolphins, etc.) – but NOT on humans. However, the mere thought of a shark attack hits three basic human terror triggers and appeals to our most deep-seated fears: of being out of our habitual element, of a hidden monster lurking somewhere out there (playing on the Great White's reputation as an ambush predator and search patroller), and of being eaten alive. Although it's clear that sharks were portrayed as monster killers long before Benchley wrote his book, or Spielberg made the film, *Jaws* is often fingered as a major culprit in giving sharks their killer image; it certainly hits all three buttons, leaving audiences aghast – but riveted.

To the three fear triggers we have to add the place of the shark in history, and the fact that we nurture a perverse yen for monsters and for horror. A visit to any fairground reveals such 'attractions' as 'House of Horrors', 'Wall of Death', 'Spooky Monsters', etc. Completely absent is any sign of 'The House of Love', 'The Happy Room' or 'Beautiful Creatures'! History, our basic fears, and our predilection for monsters will probably forever unfairly condemn sharks to being regarded as mindless killers.

In the mid-1980s marine scientists started to realise that many shark populations were under threat. As the new millennium dawned these concerns were becoming more widely accepted as fact; they were shared across the marine world and were well publicised in the media too. In 1991 the work of international expert Dr Leonard Campagno and others led to the Great White shark's being listed as protected by the South African government. This was a precautionary measure and it was the first time a shark had been given protection based on the 'precautionary principle'. In addition to South Africa, the Great White is also protected in the United States, Australia and many other countries, and in October 2004 at the CITES COP in Bangkok, the Great White was given an Appendix II listing. This listing bans all but specific, controlled, international trade monitored by CITES in Great Whites and their body parts.

The main threat to sharks was their overfishing to meet the ever-increasing demand for the eastern delicacy, shark-fin soup. The Chinese economy was booming, and a rapidly expanding – and newly affluent – middle class had an appetite for the traditional luxuries previously denied them. Sharks were the losers: once a by-catch of other fisheries, they were now being targeted in their own right as tens of millions were harvested each year, primarily for their fins.

Each headline seemed to vie with the previous one: '30 million sharks killed each year'; '70 million' and even '100 million'. Without solid baseline data, the extent of their overfishing was not known, nor how fast they were possibly being pushed to extinction in some areas. We now know that the Great White shark is particularly vulnerable to overfishing because of its late sexual maturity and its low rate of reproduction. Some suggest their worldwide numbers may have dropped to as low as 3,000.

Until the recent spate of Orca attacks on Great Whites off the Western Cape, these sharks were generally thought to have to contend with only one major predator – humans. Fatal attacks by Orcas on Great Whites had been recorded on many occasions before, but the widely held opinion was that Great Whites were nevertheless the ultimate apex predators in the marine world.

Killer whales have in the past been sighted off South Africa's coasts, but relatively rarely, and the author found only one earlier record in South Africa of Orcas attacking Great Whites (in Plettenberg Bay in 2002, when a male Orca from a group of three killed a 4-metre Great White shark). That Orcas now seem to be targeting Great Whites in South African waters is substantiated by the evidence: clusters of confirmed sightings of Port and Starboard on Dave Hurwitz' chart (see pages 110–111) that coincide with locations where Great Whites are known to spend time: False Bay, Gansbaai and Mossel Bay. It is assumed that Port and Starboard are the main culprits, but there is nothing to say that they are the only Orcas taking Great Whites in the region. For instance, another Orca nicknamed 'Stumpy' has been observed travelling with Port and Starboard, and it is logical to assume that he has learnt the same skills.

Chris Fallows believes that longline fishing is partly responsible for the reduction in Great White numbers.

For over 20 years Simon's Town-based Chris and Monique Fallows have been taking wildlife and shark enthusiasts on trips to see Great Whites. In the winter, Seal Island in False Bay is where newly weaned Cape fur seal pups first venture into the water. The sharks are waiting for them, and this area has become famous for its 'flying sharks', when Great Whites attack the seals from underneath and their upward momentum

Great Whites are now under threat from two super-
predatory mammals – humans and Orcas.

takes them clear of the water. Fallows has not only been photographing,
filming and taking people to see these amazing predators, he has also been
keeping records.

In 2004 there was a peak average of 11 shark-on-seal attacks per trip.
By 2017 the figure had dropped dramatically to 0.3 such events per trip. In
Gansbaai, Mossel Bay and False Bay, for the same 20-year period, sighting
records show peaks and troughs, but overall the trend is down. Fallows and
others believe longline fishing activity has been taking a steady toll, and
the shark nets off KwaZulu-Natal are also thought by many to be adding
to the attrition of sharks.

It is generally assumed that Port, Starboard, and maybe Stumpy
have been taking Great Whites only in the last two or three years – but
this remains an assumption. Because of Port and Starboard's collapsed
fins, they are not as easy to see as they would be with fully erect
dorsals, and until dead Great Whites started washing up on beaches,
little attention was focused on the Orcas. As Alison Towner pointed
out: 'We only know about the dead sharks found on beaches; there
must be others lying on the seabed or washed out to sea. If significant
numbers of breeding-age animals are being predated by Orcas, there
will be an impact on the population.'

Research based on photo identification over a five-year period done by Towner and the Dyer Island Conservation Trust, and published in 2013, identified 532 individual Great Whites and, with the use of a computer program, the 'open' population along South Africa's coast was extrapolated to be between 808 and 1008. Later research done by marine biologist Sara Andreotti, a postdoctoral researcher at Stellenbosch University, estimated a lesser figure of between 350 and 520.

Accurate figures are not known but longline fishing, shark nets and other human factors are negatively impacting on the population, and now Orca predation has joined the list of fatal threats facing South Africa's Great White sharks.

Unlike in South Africa, scientists elsewhere – Chris Lowe in California and Aaron MacNeil in Australia – are optimistic about their Great White populations. The Great White shark has been on our planet for hundreds of millions of years, Orcas for probably about 11 million, and humans for just 200,000 years. South Africa's Great Whites seems to be at the mercy of two super-predatory – and both much more recently evolved – mammal species.

Bronze Whaler sharks are also called Copper or Narrowtooth sharks, and their scientific name is *Carcharhinus brachyurus*. They are widely occurring but are commonly found in waters off South Africa, Australia, New Zealand, the Mediterranean and North and South America. They prefer waters above 17 degrees Centigrade and are mostly found in the top 100 metres of the water column. These sharks hunt – and are often found – in large groups, as when following the winter sardine run along the east coast of southern Africa.

Bronze Whaler females commonly grow up to 3 metres, making them bigger than males, which grow to about 2.3 metres. They are not generally considered dangerous to humans but may pose a threat in the presence of food sources. These sharks are listed as 'Near Threatened' on the IUCN Red List.

CHAPTER 15

Oceans under threat

Humans are depleting the resources on the
planet faster than they can be replaced, and are also
contributing to climate change. These actions
amount to a deadly cocktail that threatens life on
earth – a truth that has been evident for many
years, but is only now starting to get the attention
that may lead to remedial action. Failure to respond
could doom life on earth – time is of the essence.

Chris Fallows

In addition to our concerns about climate change and resource depletion are the
unknown effects of marine ecologies rebalancing, thanks to human influences.

Apex predators occupy the top feeding level in food chains. Remove the apex predators and there will be a cascade effect down the whole food chain to the bottom level.

Once the Great White sharks were no longer a permanent feature of the marine ecology in the Dyer Island area, it did not take long for Alison Towner and other scientists and observers to notice changes in the local marine ecology. The question is, to what degree are humans responsible? When does natural history become unnatural history?

Bronze Whaler sharks have always been present in the area, but it wasn't until the threat from Orcas caused the Great Whites to leave that this species seemed to increase in number and started responding to chum around ecotourism boats – the first time this had been noticed in South African waters. The arrival of a semi-resident population of 50 to 70 Bronze Whalers would certainly have some impact on the feeding chain, and this will become apparent with time.

The Great Whites in the Dyer Island area prey on the Cape fur seal colony, so the absence of the sharks means the seals need to be less vigilant. This has the knock-on effect of increasing predation by the seals, mainly the large bulls, on the African Penguin colony. Cape fur seals are not an endangered species, but the African Penguin is listed by the International Union for the Conservation of Nature (IUCN) on its Red List as 'Endangered'. This new predatory behaviour by the seals on the penguins has caused such concern that the authorities have undertaken limited and selective culling of some seal bulls, known as rogues, to ease the impact.

Abalone harvesting, now regarded as poaching due to the species' protected status, has long been practised by those in the area who make their living from the sea. The presence of Great Whites has generally had the effect of deterring poachers – not entirely, but it undoubtedly helps keep poaching in check. Once the sharks were absent or their numbers significantly reduced, it didn't take long for the abalone poachers to start taking advantage of the safer waters. Large numbers of RIBs (rigid inflatable boats) started working around Dyer Island, and as the ecotourist boats came and went, they often saw the telltale bubbles coming from divers working the seabed collecting abalone. Although the poachers' boats were clearly visible to anyone watching, and it was obvious what they were doing, up to late 2018 little effort was being made by the authorities to stop it.

A well-known resident of Shark Town, who did not want to be named, said: 'It is completely lawless out there; it's like a marine wild west and all the sheriffs have left town. Seeing those poachers in such numbers is like standing helplessly by watching while the ocean is being raped. Later the army was called in to bolster law enforcement efforts.'

The whole Great White shark ecotourism industry with its direct and indirect employment has ceased to be the reliable meal ticket it had been for many years. Some of the increase in poaching can be attributed to the safer waters, but it is also a consequence of the decline of ecotourism that has precipitated the need for an alternative pay check.

The scientific name for the abalone is *Haliotidae*, and the white abalone has been listed as 'Endangered' in the United States. In South Africa, abalone is known as 'perlemoen', taken from the Dutch meaning 'mother of pearl'. It is estimated that over the past 18 years poachers have taken at least 96 million abalone from South African waters. This rate of harvesting is considered unsustainable, and in the Dyer Island area the absence of Great Whites appears to be hastening the process of completely stripping the seabed of this valuable natural resource.

Abalone are sea snails and are at the very lower end of the chain in which Great Whites are the apex predators. That the absence of Great Whites is causing the local marine ecology to change is beyond dispute. Time may show that human influence of some kind provided the trigger for Port and Starboard's behaviour, which led to the dispersal of the sharks, and in turn to safer waters and increased abalone poaching. It looks possible, some say probable, that human meddling is present at both ends of the trophic scale.

It is almost impossible to walk too far along the sandy beach from Hermanus towards De Kelders without coming across the dead bodies of sea creatures. Seals, penguins, seabirds and others are washed up all along the beach, and even a cursory examination often reveals death has been caused by fishing net or line entanglement, oil or other pollution, propeller damage and other human factors.

Our seas are changing, and the evolving situation being studied by scientists in Walker Bay is an example of how changing seas are threatening the marine environment and impacting the lives both of the creatures that live in it and the humans that live off it. It is a constant worry for those most closely involved, who feel the immediate impact. If Shark Town's problems were unusual or unique, they could be ignored, other than by those involved. But the reality is that Shark Town's experience is being repeated in different ways and to varying degrees all over the planet. This should be of the gravest concern to us all.

The UK BBC's *Blue Planet II* is widely acknowledged as being one of the finest TV wildlife documentaries ever produced. It has been shown by TV channels all over the world, and in the last episode David Attenborough, the programme's host, spelt out the dangers of plastic pollution in the world's oceans. His observations significantly increased global awareness that we are strangling our oceans and their inhabitants with plastics. This was perhaps the most effective wake-up call yet, and Attenborough does not think it is too late to clean up our world and save it. It is up to each and every human on earth to do their bit, to prove him right, and save our seas not only for the Orcas, but for all marine species.

Epilogue

More than once when writing *Orca*, I was asked: 'What do you think will happen? Who will win?' I felt depressed every time I heard the question. Why do so many of us have to think in terms of winners and losers? Wild places – the oceans, and what's left of wilderness on land – are not football fields on which winner and loser games are being played out.

Wilfred Chivell believes the human footprint is probably present somewhere as an influence in this story, and I expect science, in one way or another, and to some degree or other, to prove him right. Rather than think of this story as a battle between two apex predators with a winner and a loser, I think of it as a scenario in which all those involved are probable losers. The increased presence of Orcas and their predation on

Great Whites may be because Orcas are losing out due to negative human impact. In this case, the Great Whites clearly lose against the Orcas, and Shark Town's humans may lose their livelihoods.

Wildlife all over the planet is struggling to live with an ever-increasing human population continuously using more land and more resources. Climate change, unsustainable use of natural resources, devastation of wildlife and other factors are all interlinked, and now require action on a global level. Failure to deal effectively with these issues is placing life on earth under threat. If the rate of despoliation continues, the ultimate loser will be the human species.

The following quotation is said to have originated from Chief Seattle in a letter to US President Franklin Pierce in 1855. The quote has been credited, discredited, discussed and researched for years, but if we fail to arrest the rampant devastation of our planet, it may turn out to be a relevant comment: 'If all the beasts were gone, man would die from loneliness of spirit, for whatever happens to the beast, happens to man. All things are connected. Whatever befalls the earth, befalls the sons of earth.'

The dorsal fins of male Orcas can measure up to 1.8 metres.

Hennie Otto

POST SCRIPT

As the clock ticked on into 2019 it became increasingly apparent that the new reality of life on the Shark Town coast was, at best, fragile. This fragility applied not only to life on land, but also to marine ecosystems. History and scientific research will eventually define the extent to which Port and Starboard were responsible for the Great Whites abruptly and intermittently moving away from the Dyer Island area. However, as time passes, fears continue to grow that the general depletion of the species is having a more severe impact on South African Great White numbers than was previously acknowledged. Port and Starboard may be the trigger that causes the dispersal, but they are dispersing a population that is being depleted anyway due to a range of hostile human activities mentioned in Chapter 13 – longlining, shark nets, pollution, overfishing, etc.

Longliners operating out of Cape Town have recently been joined by two new licence holders working out of Mossel Bay – and specifically targeting shark species. They work mostly between Mossel Bay and Cape Agulhas, so at the southwest end of their range they are fishing right on the doorstep of Dyer Island's Great White sharks. For Great Whites, South Africa's east coast is a highway from the Cape all the way to Mozambique. The arrival of two new longliners has made the road that much more dangerous. While believing that longline fisheries are certainly impacting on Great Whites, Chivell and Fallows point out that all fisheries that take prey species from the ocean must eventually have a negative impact on the entire food chain. Chivell cites the example of an experimental octopus fishery in False Bay, which he thinks has a significant impact on smaller shark species in that area, in turn impacting on the Great Whites at the top of that food chain.

Brenda du Toit, Wilfred Chivell's assistant, remarked that she was frustrated with foreign newspapers ringing up every time they heard the Great Whites had disappeared again, and then writing up and disseminating their reports widely for a readership ever hungry for shark-related news. She pointed out that every time this happened it had a negative effect on visitor numbers, and this 'news' approach was neither accurate nor sensible – and was often rapidly overtaken by changing circumstances. On one occasion a UK news story about the disappearance of the sharks had actually been published the same day Great Whites had reappeared!

In Chapter 12 Dave Caravias posed the question as to why tourists would want to come on holiday to an area in which water might run out, there was civil unrest and riots, and the sharks had gone. When Dave made this remark the questions were valid, and the concerns were definitely affecting tourist numbers. However, in the first six months of 2019 there was no serious civil unrest or riots in the Hermanus and Gansbaai area; national elections in May did not produce any startling or dangerous results, and most people hoped that peace was now in the air. Water reserves had held up all through the previous summer and were being effectively managed. Great Whites came and went, Bronze Whalers plugged the shark gaps, and tourists continued to come to Shark Town. Early summer 2018 had probably seen the height of the gloom, and by the middle of 2019 pragmatism and positive developments meant that those in Shark Town's shark ecotourism sector were less fearful about their future, having learnt to adapt to the new realities.

Then on Sunday 26th May 2019 Dave Hurwitz of the Simon's Town Boat Company posted the following on his Facebook page:

'Port & Starboard have now discovered Seal Island in False Bay! We've seen them close to the island before, but they showed little interest in surveying the area for a potential meal and always moved straight inshore. Presumably this is because they were aware that Seal Island in the past didn't have a high aggregation of Cow sharks. Recently this has changed though; with the desertion of the White sharks, Cow sharks have relocated there after being displaced from their regular localities due to increased Orca predations on them.

And the Orcas certainly had a feast today – an estimated 10 Cow sharks were consumed during the 5+ hours that Port & Starboard worked the area.'

On the 29th May I spoke to Dave Hurwitz to confirm the sighting, and while we were on the phone he was at Seal Island watching Port and Starboard swimming near his boat. On the 26th there had been another three boats near Dave watching the action at Seal Island; he confirmed that the estimate of 10 dead Cow sharks was based on observations shared by all those on the scene, and he was fairly confident of its accuracy. As far as I am aware this is the first time that predations by Port and Starboard were actually witnessed. News, especially bad news, travels fast, and on Monday 26th May Shark Town cage-diving operators were made aware of Port and Starboard's attacks while they were happening.

Thus far, only Great Whites and Cow sharks seem to have been on the Orcas' menu. Shark Town's operators hoped it would stay that way and Bronze Whalers would not also become targets.

The story that unfolds in *Orca* links many separate but related occurrences and animal species. It shows the essential interconnectedness of life, and how every action produces a

Dave Caravias

reaction. This is true everywhere and in every field of life, but nowhere is it in sharper focus than for those who live close to nature and operate by its rhythms.

Making a living from the sea has never been easy. Wilfred Chivell and Brian McFarlane will readily admit that life was much tougher when they were young men trying to live off fishing and diving for diamonds. They acknowledge that Great Whites gave Shark Towners nearly two decades of easier living before the new uncertainties kicked in. By and large, the people of Shark Town have survived, are learning to adapt, and will continue to survive. In an uncertain world I believe that is a certainty.

Many Sevengill (Cow) sharks were killed by Port and Starboard off Seal Island in False Bay in May 2019.

Acronyms

CITES   Convention on International Trade in Endangered Species
CMS   Convention on Migratory Species
DEA   Department of Environmental Affairs
DICT   Dyer Island Conservation Trust
HWC   Human-Wildlife Conflict
IUCN   International Union for the Conservation of Nature
NGO   Non-Governmental Organisation
NPO   Not-for-Profit Organisation
NSRI   National Sea Rescue Institute
PCBs   Polychlorinated biphenyls

Useful websites

Centre for Whale Research – **www.whaleresearch.com**
Cetacean Society International – **www.csiwhalesalive.org**
CITES – **www.cites.org**
DICT – **www.dict.org.za**
Great White Shark Tours – **www.sharkcagediving.net**
Marine Dynamics – **www.sharkwatchsa.com**
Orca Lab – **www.orcalab.org**
Richard Peirce – **www.peirceshark.com**
Shark Bookings – **www.sharkbookings.com**
Shark Trust – **www.sharktrust.org**
The Roundhouse – **www.theroundhouse.co.za**
Whale Rescue – **www.whale-rescue.org**
Save Our Seas Foundation – **www.saveourseas.com**

The curled-over dorsal fin is a giveaway in the midst of a dramatic splash.

Wilfred Chivell

Dave Caravias

People are the major threat to the continued existence of Great White sharks;
Orcas are recent participants in what is already a significant onslaught.